FACE TO FACE
WITH THE
TURIN SHROUD

FACE TO FACE WITH THE TURIN SHROUD

Edited by Peter Jennings

First published in Great Britain in 1978 by
MAYHEW-McCRIMMON LTD
Great Wakering   Essex   England
&
A. R. MOWBRAY & CO. LTD.
Oxford   England

ISBN 0 85597 266 1
ISBN 0 264 66538 4

Printed by Mayhew-McCrimmon Ltd

Acknowledgements

Face to Face with the Turin Shroud would not have been possible without the magnificent co-operation afforded to me by each of the distinguished contributors, who all completed their manuscripts in a very short space of time, some at considerable personal inconvenience.

I owe a tremendous debt of gratitude to the Revd David Sox, the dynamic General Secretary of The British Society For The Turin Shroud, (73, Chatsworth Court, Pembroke Road, London, W8), for all his advice and many helpful suggestions, particularly at the start of the project and also for lending all the photographs. Those by Giuseppe Enrie are used by courtesy of Salesian Publications.

I should like to express my grateful thanks to Professor Philip McNair and to Dr John Robinson for all their help and constant encouragement throughout the editing of the manuscripts. My thanks also go to Mr Karl McIlwaine and his wife Gill, for their help in checking the manuscripts; and to my brother-in-law, Mr Bob Newitt, for his meticulous reading and correcting of all the proofs.

Finally, I should like to express my heartfelt love to my wife, Stella, for all her patience, understanding and support throughout the preparation of the book, from its conception to its completion.

Christ Jesus, who, though he was in the form of God, did not count equality with God a thing to be grasped, but emptied himself, taking the form of a servant, being born in the likeness of men. And being found in human form he humbled himself and became obedient unto death, even death on a cross.

Therefore God has highly exalted him and bestowed on him the name which is above every name, that at the name of Jesus every knee should bow, in heaven and on earth and under the earth, and every tongue confess that Jesus Christ is Lord, to the glory of God the Father.

(Philippians 2.5-11)

Contents

Foreword

Much of my work is connected with the popularisation of archaeology and history; so you might say that I am in the 'relics business' myself. But my approach to this fascinating and thought-provoking book about the Turin Shroud is, I must declare at the outset, that of a sceptic, in the original sense of the word – a disciple of Pyrrhonism, the doctrine that certainty of knowledge is unattainable. Nonetheless, there is nothing I enjoy more than an historical mystery, or indeed a mystery of any kind; and the Turin Shroud is surely one of the greatest mysteries of all time.

It is a measure of its compelling appeal as a mystery that it has even given rise to a new word in the English language which has not yet percolated into the dictionaries – 'Sindonology'. Etymologically it derives from the Greek word *sindon*, meaning 'fine cloth', taken up into Italian as *sindone*, where it is specifically applied to the 'fine cloth' known as the Turin Shroud. Hence 'Sindonology', and hence 'Sindonologist' for all those scholars and enthusiasts who have devoted their attention to the problem of the Shroud and who are even now, as this book is being published, gathered in Turin for a rare exposition of the Shroud and the Symposium dedicated to it. It is a subject which arouses profound passions in people, from those who want to believe that on the Shroud are miraculously imprinted the images, back and front, of the crucified Christ, to those who vehemently deny its authenticity. Indeed, only six years ago someone twice broke into the chapel in Turin in which the Shroud is kept and attempted to set fire to it. Whatever one may think of the Shroud, it is clearly not something to be taken lightly.

The nature and the extent of the mystery of the Shroud is most lucidly and impartially indicated in the essays that comprise this book. They make compelling reading, covering all the major aspects of the story of the Shroud and the attempts to apply scientific techniques to its examination.

There are two crucial problems connected with it. One is that it has no historical or documentary provenance before the middle of the 14th century; nothing at all is known about it before it turned

11

up in rather enigmatic circumstances in an age when so-called holy relics from the early Christian period were very big business indeed – and it was vigorously denounced as a forgery by eminent prelates at the time. The second is that scientific examination of the Shroud (admittedly not using the very latest techniques available) has failed so far to produce any definitive answers. The cloth of the Shroud is of a kind not inconsistent with a Palestinian provenance, and not inconsistent with a 1st century AD date – but that is not to say that it actually *is* from 1st century AD Palestine. Similarly, examination of some selected fibres of the cloth has indicated that no pigment or paint or organic fluid like blood caused the ghostly images on the Shroud; so what did? It has been suggested that they are a kind of scorch mark, which might have been caused by an instant's flash of radiation! These ghostly images, it is suggested, are intrinsically unfakeable. I would have thought that modern scientific techniques should be capable of deciding this particular question one way or another; the fact that it has so far defied analysis does not mean that it is unanalysable.

The Church has always been chary of trying to 'prove' the unprovable by exposing relics to scientific examination, or encouraging belief in them. There seem to me to be two perfectly valid reasons for this.

In the first place, 'science' is by no means infallible. It is capable of making the most fearful blunders in its evaluation of evidence. One need only think of the considerable corrections that have had to be made in archaeological circles to the 'absolute' dates for organic material supplied by radiocarbon 14 testing. C14 dating, which was developed just after the War, was hailed as the instant solution to all problems of relative dating in archaeology, and earned its discoverer, Willard F. Libby, a Nobel prize. Now, through the newer technique of tree-ring dating, C14 dates are having to be modified, or 'calibrated' as the archaeological jargon has it, up to a margin of 2,000 years in some early periods. Similarly, the technique of thermoluminescence, whereby pottery could be given an absolute date, was hailed as another revolutionary solution; but some of the dates produced by the thermoluminescence technique are so bizarre that there are clearly problems still attendant on the method. So one really does have to be rather wary about believing the sometimes exaggerated claims of what scientific technique and scientific analysis are capable of. Spectacular forgeries like the Piltdown skull and the artefacts from Glozel remained for a long time impervious to scientific investigation, because they were bolstered by scholars who laid their professional reputations on the line in defence of their authenticity: science is ultimately only as good as the scientist.

Secondly, there is nothing more damaging than evidence which is exposed as a fake or a hoax – damaging not simply in respect of the article itself, but of the whole field of knowledge or belief with which it is associated. If we look at the world of the Vikings, for instance, there have been some sensational fakes and forgeries designed to 'prove' that the Vikings discovered and explored North America in the early middle ages. The Kensington Stone, with its ludicrous parody of a Swedish runic inscription, emerged on cue in the 1890s in one of the most Scandinavian states of the USA, soon after public interest had been whetted by an epic voyage from Norway to America in a replica of the celebrated Gokstad ship. The ill-fated Vinland Map came on to the anti-quarian market at a time when scholarly interest in the Saga texts about the Norse discovery of Vinland was at its height. The only effect of these wretched forgeries was to cast doubt and even con-tumely on all other evidence of the period – particularly the docu-mentary sources themselves. In the field of faith, it is surely better to allow the pious and the devout to believe what they like without making any official claims about the authenticity of relics or miracles.

If the Turin Shroud is a forgery, or a work of art, no one has yet been able to show how it was done. This does not prove that it was not done. There is good reason to believe that no 14th century artist could have the extraordinary anatomical knowledge and artistic technique to create so accurately the image of a man savagely tortured in almost exactly the same way as described in the Gospels. But has sufficient attention been paid to the possibility that the forgery is much later? It was only when the Shroud was exposed to photography in 1898, for instance, that the majestic features of the face on the Shroud were first recognised. Could there conceivably have been a tampering with the cloth at that time?

I raise all these points not because I believe that the Turin Shroud *is* a fraud, either modern or medieval, or even a work of art. I simply do not know. I find it fascinating and genuinely amazing; almost uncanny, in fact. But one should not allow the wish for authenticity to sway judgement. In times of uncertainty, people tend to *need* a token of this kind, a life-line for their faith, something paranormal or supernatural in tangible form to reinforce the super-natural claims of their religion. When faced with the apparently irrational, people sometimes become rather irrational themselves.

I suppose it is not impossible that in fifty years time, with ever-improving scientific techniques, some pioneer will have demonstrated beyond reasonable doubt that the Shroud is a perfectly normal artefact, with a perfectly normal explanation, and people will be saying 'Do you remember all those Turin Shroud freaks who called themselves Sindonologists and actually thought it was miraculous?' I don't know. It could well be. On the other hand it could just as well not be, and the next generation will be left with this most teasing and tantalising of historical mysteries that goes right to the heart of our knowing. In a way, I would be reluctant to see the mystery definitively solved — but that is only because I am a true sceptic!

Meanwhile, for anyone interested in mysteries, and specifically in this particular mystery, these scholarly and sober essays bring the story right up to date. By the time the Turin Symposium (7-8 October 1978) is over, they might be *out* of date again; for the story of the Turin Shroud does not stand still.

Magnus Magnusson

Glasgow, August 1978

No 1 *And Front Cover*
**The mysterious and haunting
face on the Turin Shroud as
revealed by negative plate.
Photograph taken by
Giuseppe Enrie, in 1931.**

No 2.
The face on the Turin Shroud seen in positive. Photograph taken by Giovanni Battista Judica-Cordiglia, in 1969.

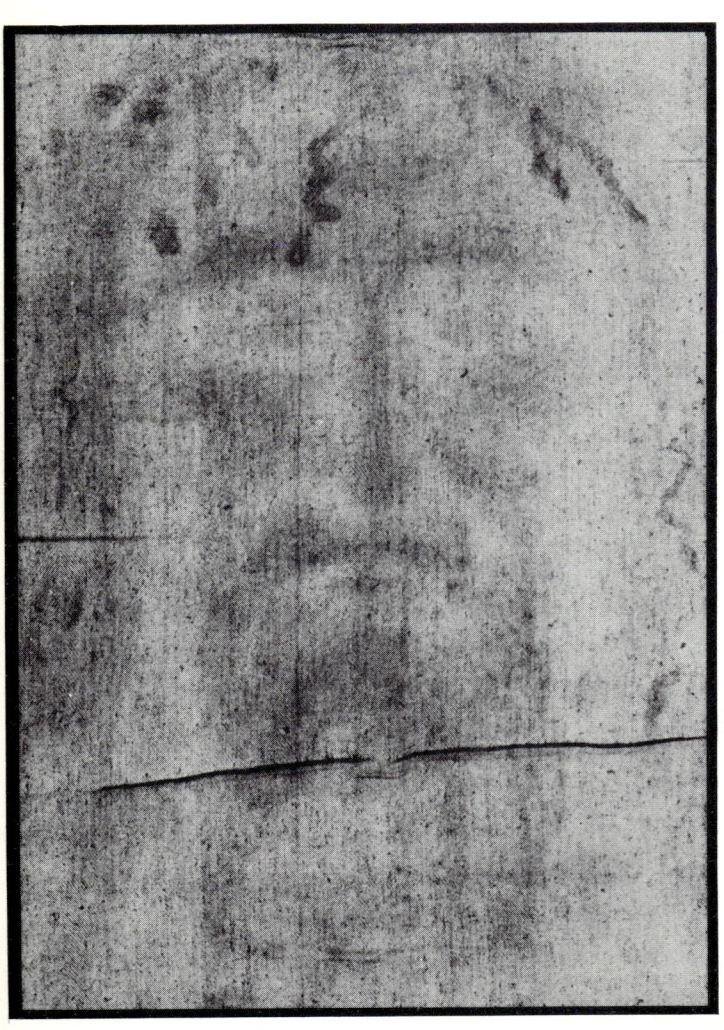

No 3.
The face on the Turin Shroud seen in negative. Photograph taken by Giovanni Battista Judica-Cordiglia, in 1969.

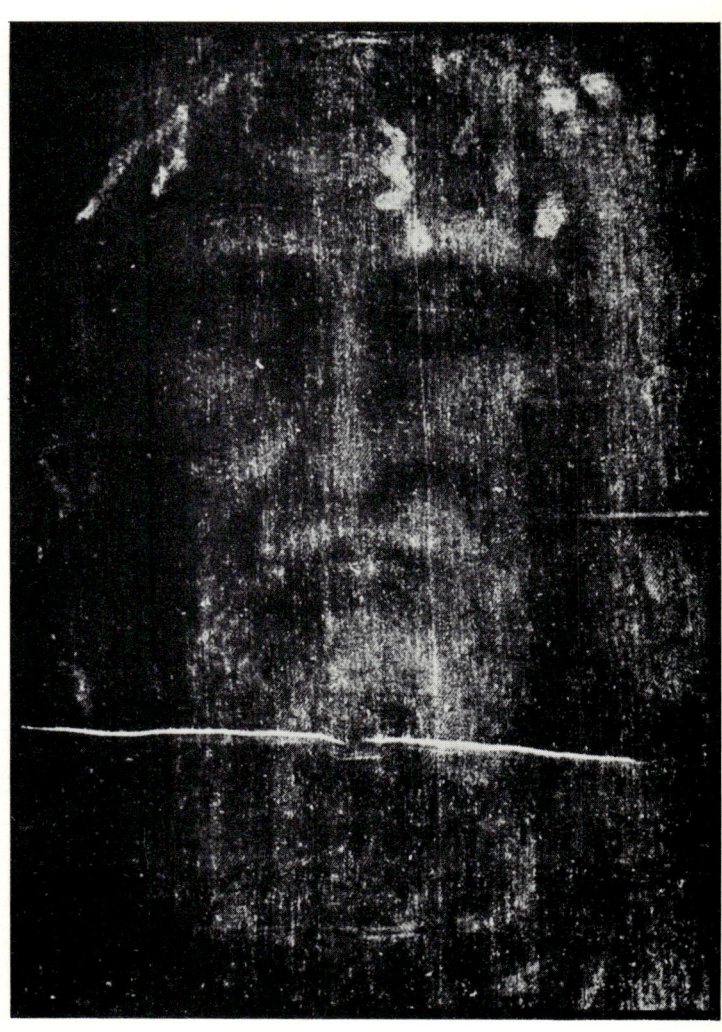

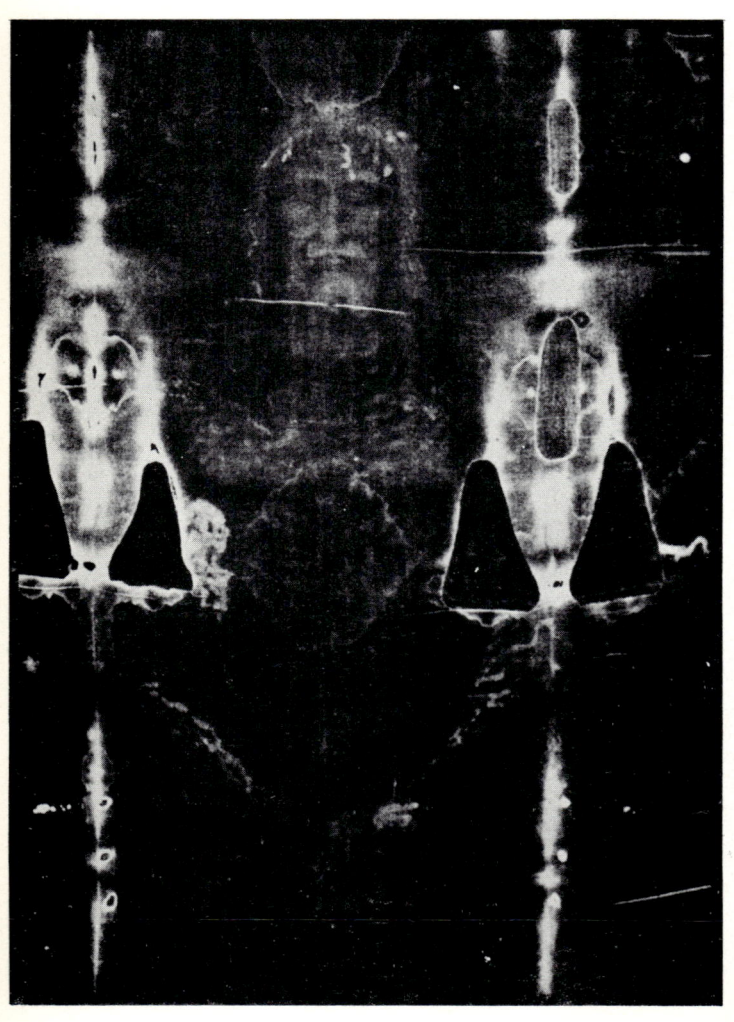

No. 5
The back of the image on the
Turin Shroud seen in negative
Photograph taken by
Giuseppe Enrie, in 1931.

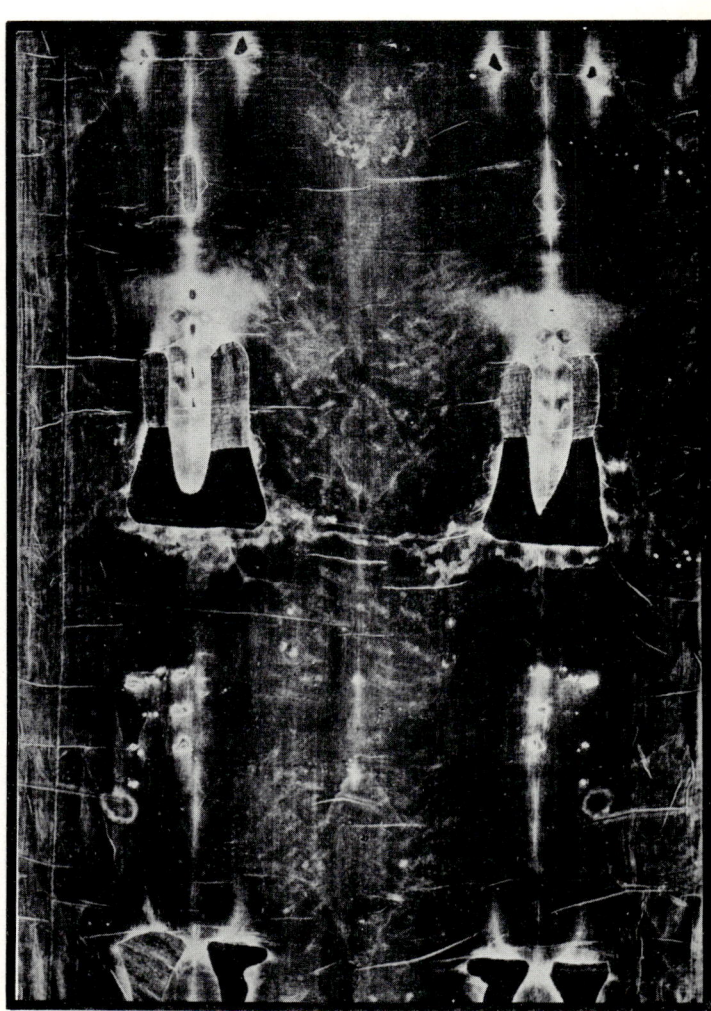

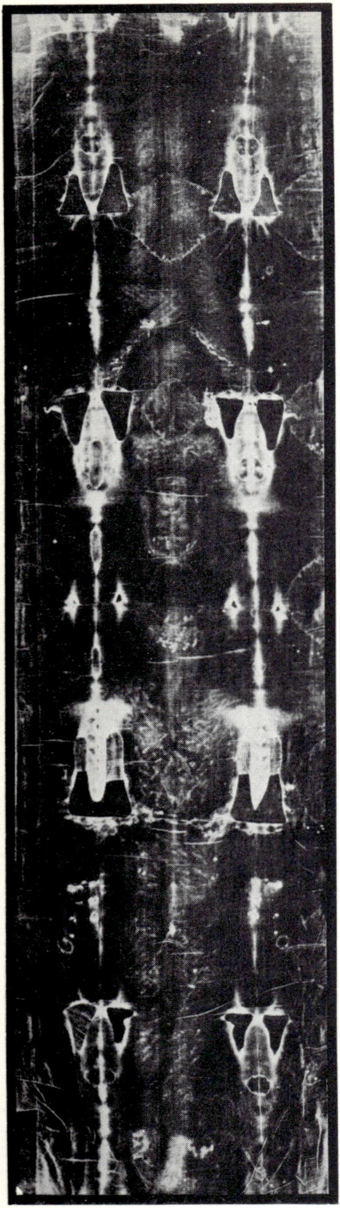

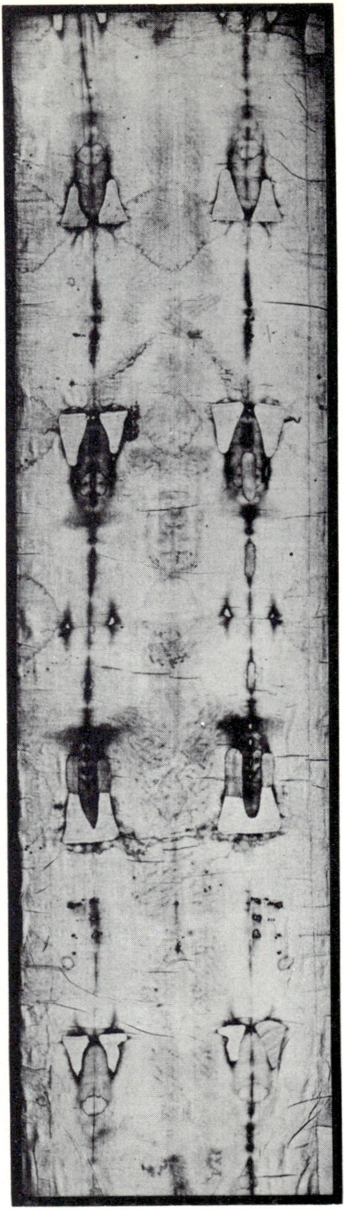

No 6. *(Facing Page)*
The full length image on the Turin Shroud, both positive and negative. Photographs taken by Giuseppe Enrie, in 1931.

No 7.
Relief image of the face on the Turin Shroud produced by Dr. John Jackson and Doctor Eric Jumper through VP–8 Image Analyser.

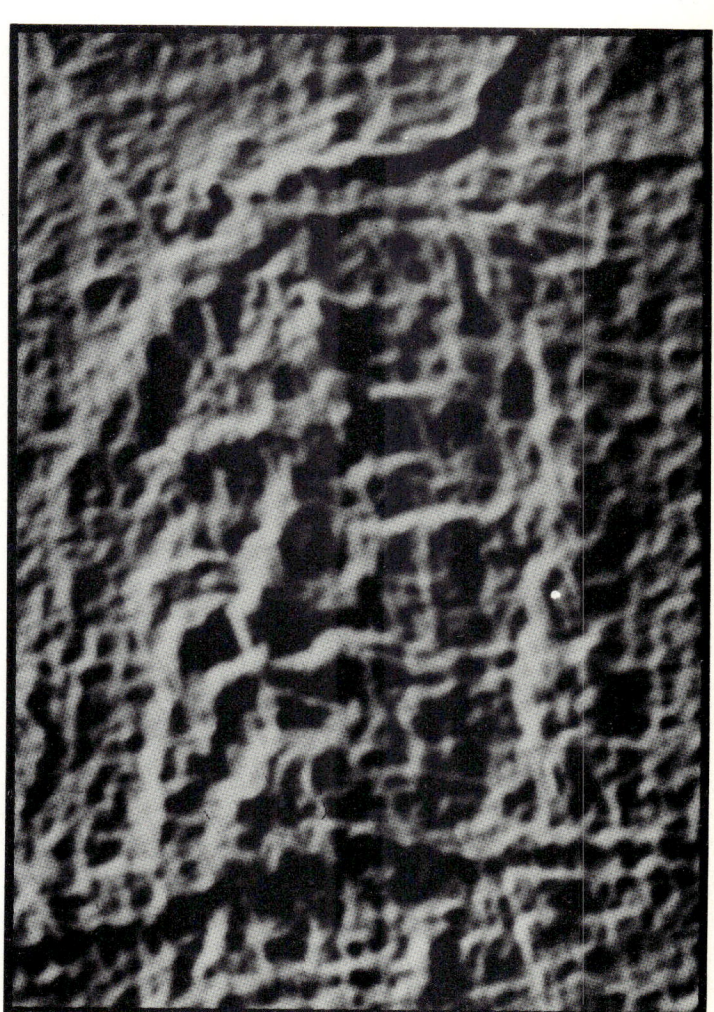

No 8. *(Top picture)*
The weave of the Turin Shroud as seen in magnification. (Courtesy British Society for the Turin Shroud)

No 9. *(Lower picture)*
One of the two samples taken from the Turin Shroud in 1973 for analysis by Belgian textile expert, Professor Gilbert Raes. (Courtesy British Society for the Turin Shroud.)

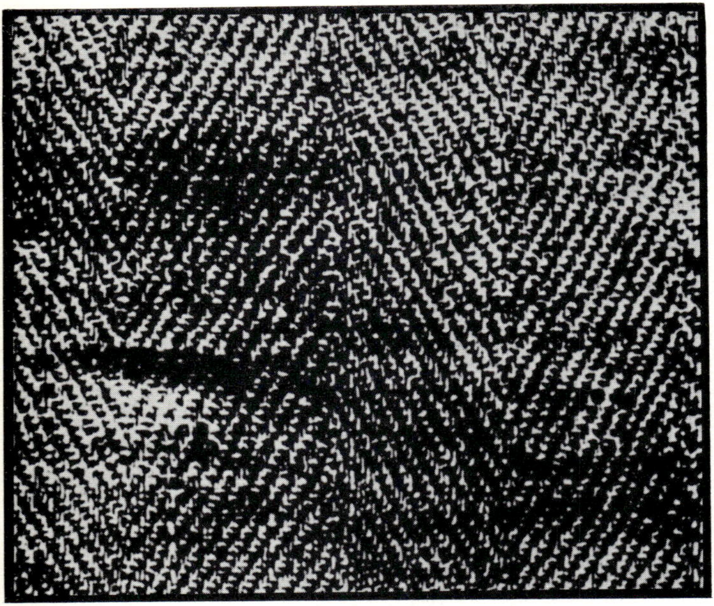

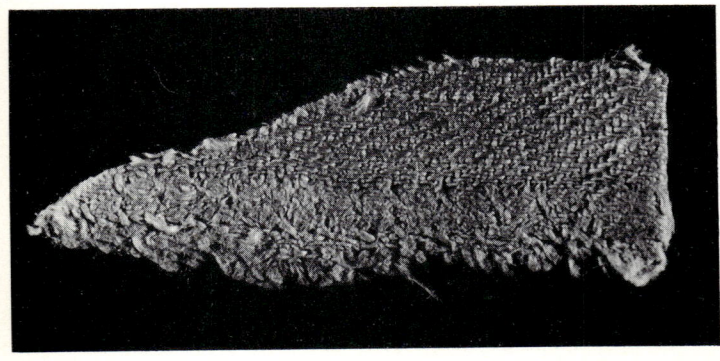

Editor's Preface

The Turin Shroud has been an object of mystery and fascination to Christians for centuries, and this book seeks to bring the reader face to face with the haunting image on this piece of ivory-coloured linen cloth. In his chapter the Revd H. David Sox describes the tensions that have existed between the Turin Authorities and those people who want to bring the Shroud to the test. Ex-King Umberto II, its owner, who now lives in Portugal, has stated that he has no objection to letting competent research go as far as it can in exploring the mysteries of the image on the Cloth. News of the death of Pope Paul VI was announced as these words were being written, so it is fitting to record that he was responsible for breaking down some of the resistance in Turin to the testing of the Shroud.

What are we to make of this piece of old linen cloth? Does it bear the imprint of Jesus Christ? Many people believe that it does. Mr John Walsh ended the Preface of his book *The Shroud*, published in 1964, by saying: 'Only this much is certain. The Shroud of Turin is either the most awesome and instructive relic of Jesus Christ in existence – or it is one of the most ingenious, most unbelievably clever products of the human mind and hand on record. It is one or the other; there is no middle ground.'

The Shroud has no authenticated history between the crucifixion and the fourteenth century. Professor Philip McNair disagrees with Mr Ian Wilson's idea that the Edessa Image and the Turin Shroud are one and the same thing and writes: 'His hypothesis, presented with a wealth of circumstantial evidence, is as attractive as it is unconvincing; for, although it would have explained so much, it is fraught with difficulties which many critical readers will find insuperable.'

Remarkably the Shroud has suffered little damage during its history. It was caught in a fire at Chambéry in December 1532, and this has provided some interesting evidence as the scorch marks caused by the fire have been found to be consistent with the strange markings on the cloth and provide the only clue as to how they got there.

17

These marks are not caused by paint or any pigment. They have not penetrated the linen fibres, as paint would have done, nor do they appear on the back of the cloth and scientific investigation has detected no traces of actual blood-substance on the Shroud. Is it possible that a burst of radiant heat from the moment when Jesus Christ was raised from the dead, left its imprint on the Shroud?

The conglomeration and wealth of historical, scientific, medical and biblical evidence presented in this book all points to the authenticity of the Turin Shroud. However, despite the fact that the figure on the cloth has been scourged, executed and pierced in the manner described of Jesus of Nazareth in the four Gospels, there will *never* be any absolute proof that this is the Shroud in which his dead body was put when he was taken down from the Cross and laid in the tomb.

The Rt Revd Dr John A. T. Robinson, one of the foremost New Testament scholars of our day, asks the vital question: 'What *difference* would it make to us if it were genuine?' Christianity does not need such proofs as the Turin Shroud but perhaps we do in order to help us out of the complacency of our agnosticism or to strengthen our latent faith in Jesus Christ.

The ultimate challenge of the Shroud is to one's personal convictions in the light of the many and varied sources of evidence. These six compellingly cogent essays are offered as a stimulus to further study. But what is clear from any examination of the facts is that *if* this Shroud bears the marks of authenticity that these distinguished writers claim, then the marks of nail, spear, and crown of thorns, speak of a far greater cost of suffering in God's identification in Christ with a suffering world, for its rescue and redemption, than any words can tell.

Peter Jennings

Feast of the Transfiguration 1978

The Editor

PETER JENNINGS, born in London in 1947, is a freelance journalist who specializes in Religious Affairs, and is actively committed to the cause of ecumenism. He has done research for ATV religious programmes *Saints Alive* and *Something Different*; and contributes to many religious publications including *The Tablet*.

A practising Roman Catholic, Peter Jennings who is married to an Evangelical Anglican, acts in a part-time capacity as Press Officer for the Anglican Bishop of Birmingham, the Rt Revd Hugh Montefiore. He and his wife Stella, live in the Harborne district of Birmingham.

Chapter One
The Shroud and History: fantasy, fake or fact?
Philip McNair

The subject of this book is a mysterious length of old cloth preserved in Turin Cathedral. It has been called various names in successive ages by different people. When I first felt its fascination more than twenty years ago, we non-Italians usually referred to it by its traditional Latin name of *Sudarium Taurinensis,* or sweat-cloth of Turin; but other names are more popular today. In Turin and the rest of Italy it is known to millions of Catholics as 'la Santa Sindone' or just 'la Sindone', and to an ever-increasing number of English-speaking people throughout Christendom and beyond it is becoming known as 'the Holy Shroud of Turin', 'the Turin Shroud' – or simply 'the Shroud'. There is something apt and familiar about the simplicity of that monosyllable, and an unspoken claim lies in its juxtaposition with the definite article. Other shrouds are preserved in other places, of course, just as there were other dukes alive in the days of Wellington: but this one – paradoxically – is unique. *The Shroud.* And that is what we shall call it here, although by giving it this functional name we have already begged the central question of its existence, for there is no record that this length of old cloth ever enveloped a lifeless body.

When is a shroud not a shroud? – when it's a fake: and there are far too many pious frauds in the history of the Christian Church for us to accept every treasured relic at its face value. Therefore the subject of this first chapter is the Shroud and history: how shall we explain that teasing absence of reliable records about its origins and provenance? In the tangled skein of legend, hypothesis and wishful thinking which wraps it round, where shall we separate fantasy from fact? When all is said and done, what options remain open to us as we are brought face to face with the Turin Shroud? But before we tackle the vexed question of its authenticity, let us define what it is that we are facing – and here we might as well begin with the verifiable and undisputed facts.

This length of ivory-coloured cloth measures 14 feet 3 inches by 3 feet 7 inches, or 4.36 metres by 1.10 metre. Its exact age has not yet been determined, but it is at least six hundred years old, and there is nothing in its fabric or weave to invalidate the claim that its manufacture is of the first century AD. From the purely textile angle it can be described as a three-to-one herring-bone twill, the material being linen with a small admixture of cotton (as the Belgian Professor Gilbert Raes reported in 1976 after his microscopic examination of carefully selected and extracted threads of it in his textile laboratory at Ghent University).

The presence of cotton fibres in the weave is considered by experts to be conclusive in ruling out a European provenance for the fabric of the Shroud, since cotton was not grown or used in Europe in any possible epoch of the manufacture of this cloth. But it is entirely consonant with a Palestinian provenance, as the fibres are of the *Gossypium Herbaceum* variety which is cultivated in the Middle East. The total absence of wool in the Shroud's composition is instructive to anyone versed in the Mosaic Law with its prohibition of textile mixture, for Leviticus 19.19 commands: 'Thou shalt not let thy cattle gender with a diverse kind: thou shalt not sow thy field with mingled seed: neither shall a garment mingled of linen and woollen come upon thee.' The presence of even one wool fibre would have excluded this cloth from ever having been a Jewish burial shroud.

But to describe this artefact as a length of linen cloth would be as inadequate as to describe Leonardo da Vinci's *Mona Lisa* as an oblong wooden panel in a frame. There are marks on the Turin Shroud. Some (the most obvious) are accidental and easily explained. Other are remedial and present no problem. But the central markings seem to be intentional and baffle all natural explanation. The accidental marks are burns and singes caused by molten silver in a fire which broke out in the Sainte-Chapelle at Chambéry on the night of 3-4, December 1532. The remedial marks are triangular linen patches applied to the worst of these burns by the Poor Clares of Sainte-Claire-en-Ville in April 1534. But the marks down the centre of the Shroud's length are mysterious in the extreme. Quite what they are, or how they were caused, no one can honestly say, least of all the scientists who have examined them. They are not marks caused by paint or any pigment. They have not penetrated the linen fibres, as paint would have done, nor have they insinuated themselves between the fibres, nor do they appear on the back of the cloth.

These marks have shape and figure. At first sight they might suggest two ghostly brass-rubbings of some medieval knight bereft of armour. On closer inspection they are seen faintly but perceptibly to represent the naked body – both back and front – of a mature bearded male with long hair who would have stood about 5 feet 11 inches tall and weighed in the region of $12\frac{1}{2}$ stone, or 175 pounds. It appears that he has been laid supine on one half of the cloth, while the other half has been doubled back to cover him from face to feet, so that the two life-size images lie head to head down the centre of the Shroud.

This Shroud-Man has seemingly suffered several sorts of physical violence. Apart from the abrasions, bruises and swellings which minute investigation reveals, there are apparent traces of various and distinct blood-flows: from the head, wrist, feet, and (most marked) from the side – from what is evidently an incision between the fifth and sixth rib. His back, from the shoulders down to the ankles, is liberally spattered with more than a hundred dumb-bell shaped scores where the skin has apparently been broken by flagellation, consonant with the application of a leaded whip, such as the Roman *flagrum*.

Painstaking scientific examination by a team of Italian haematologists in the last ten years has detected no trace of actual blood-substance on the cloth; but, by the same token, forensic experts have detected no trace of any natural or artificial matter which might have been used to simulate blood, such as Hollywood employs in filming a Western. Art has not improved on Nature. Here again there is no pigment, no seepage, no penetration of the linen fibres, and this established fact is one of the most baffling features of the Shroud. Yet the representation of the various blood-flows on the cloth is, from the forensic and physiological points of view, of a quite unusual degree of verisimilitude.

Now it seems to me otiose, if not ridiculous, to spend time arguing (as some leading sindonologists, such as Giulio Ricci or José-Luis Carreño Etxeandia, argue) about the identity of the man represented on the Turin Shroud. Whether it is genuine or a fake, the representation is obviously of Jesus Christ. If the figure is a fake, then the craftsman who faked it has represented the body of a man who has been mocked, scourged, executed and pierced in the manner described in the four Gospels – with one significant variant, which we shall discuss later. He has manifestly intended to portray the Jesus of Nazareth who 'suffered under Pontius Pilate, was crucified, dead, and buried', and has made an extraordinarily accurate job of it down to the least detail. If, on the other hand, the figure is authentic, it can only be Jesus for three good reasons: first, because it is most unlikely that the shrouds of any other crucified men – mainly slaves, peasants and crooks – would either have been of this quality or have been considered worth preserving; secondly, because of the thousands of victims of crucifixion which history records, only one is known to have suffered both wounds to the head (consonant with a spiky cap being pressed down upon the cranium) and the side (compatible with a deep jab from a Roman lance) as we see represented on the Shroud; and thirdly, because this man – although demonstrably crucified – has not suffered the *crurifragium,* or breaking of the leg-bones with a heavy mallet, which was an almost invariable concomitant of crucifixion. The Shroud-Man is Jesus Christ or nobody.

Except for the duration of the Second World War (when it was hidden high up in the Southern Italian Province of Avellino in the crypt of the Abbey of Montevergine, which houses a companion image of the Mother of Jesus), the Shroud has remained for the last four hundred years at Turin. It was brought there from Chambéry in September 1578 (hence its exposition throughout the month of September 1978 and the date of the publication of this book), ostensibly to shorten the journey of the Cardinal Archbishop of Milan, St Charles Borromeo (1538-84), who wished to venerate it, but more probably as part of a political move on the part of its owner, Duke Emanuele Filiberto of Savoy (1528-80), who was planning to transfer his capital from Chambéry to Turin.

Since 1694 it has been preserved in a chapel specially built for it between the apse of the Cathedral of San Giovanni Battista and the Royal Palace, known as both the Cappella Reale and the Cappella della Santa Sindone. This shrine is the work of the Theatine architect, Guarino Guarini of Modena (1624-83), and was commissioned by Duke Vittorio Amedeo II (1666-1732), the first King of Sardinia. The bold dome of this impressive black marble *rotonda* is 195 feet high, and soars beyond the top of most internal photographs. The Shroud – when not exposed – is kept rolled up round a pole inside a silvered wooden reliquary behind a grille above the altar. Although jealously guarded and protected by asbestos, it has been the target of pyromania even in this decade: on 1, October 1972 some acrobatic Herostratus climbed over the palace roof, broke into Guarini's chapel through the dome and tried to set fire to Christendom's most precious relic, repeating his gesture twenty days later. (Iconoclasm is alive and well.)

The Shroud belongs by hereditary right to the head of the House of Savoy, who is at present ex-King Umberto II, an exile in Portugal; but its *de facto* curator is the Cardinal Archbishop of

Turin, Monsignor Anastasio Ballastrero. Before 1978 there have been no more than two public expositions of it this century, apart from a brief display for an Italian television programme on Friday, 23 November 1973. The first was in 1931, to mark the marriage of Umberto, then the hereditary Prince, and the second was in 1933, to celebrate the supposed nineteenth centenary of Christ's crucifixion. Even during the last century the number of times the Shroud was exposed could be counted on the fingers of one hand, but throughout the eighteenth century it was exposed once a year on 3 May, the day of the Invention of the Cross. It was brought out in 1804 for the visit of Pope Pius VII to Turin, and in 1815 to celebrate that Pontiff's return to Italy from French captivity; but for the next three or four generations it was shown to the public only when a hereditary Prince of the Royal House of Savoy got married.

So it came about that twenty months after the future King Vittorio Emanuele III had married the Montenegran Princess Elena Petrović-Njegoš in October 1896, the occasion was celebrated retrospectively by an exposition of the Shroud which lasted eight days in May 1898 and was intended to coincide with the fiftieth anniversary of the *Statuto* of the nascent Kingdom of Italy. This was the most important public showing in the Shroud's eventful career, and was to prove a watershed in its history. For at last the sacred relic came face to face with modern science in the shape of a camera, operated by the persistent if amateur hands of a Turin lawyer called Secondo Pia (1855-1941). He was an enthusiastic photographer, and had spent a small fortune on his hobby. From about 1876 he had been getting pretty good results, developing his exposures at home from the glass plates which were then in use; in fact he had been elected President of the Turin Photo Club (Associazione degli Amatori della Fotografia di Torino).

When Secondo Pia heard about the proposed exposition of the Shroud, he conceived the novel idea of photographing it. But the idea did not appeal at all to its owner, King Umberto I; to him it seemed an act of sacrilege, and the Chairman of the Committee for Sacred Art, Baron Antonio Manno, had to overcome some stubborn resistance in persuading him to allow it. But finally the royal permission was granted, and Pia set about preparing for his unprecedented task.

There were some formidable obstacles to overcome. About a million people were expected to file past the Shroud, and the photographer would have to get the Cathedral to himself and his assistants in order to set up his elaborate equipment. There were only two times possible for the operation: either before 3 o'clock on the afternoon of 25 May, or late in the evening of 28 May. Pia settled for the first of the two. But there was no electricity in the Cathedral, and even if there had been, nobody then had much experience in the use of electricity in taking indoor photographs. He toyed with the idea of relaying light from the *piazza* by a series of looking-glasses, but gave it up for technical reasons and decided on a dynamo and lamps. Since the relic was to be exposed horizontally at a considerable height above the ground, he had to construct a platform that would run on rails – portable tracks which he would have to introduce into the Cathedral. Time was of the essence and, if anything went wrong, the whole operation would have to be scrapped.

To cut a long and exciting story short (a story, by the way, told by Pia himself in his *Memoria sulla riproduzione fotografica della santissima Sindone,* written in 1907 and published in *Sindon* in April 1960), at the first attempt something did go wrong. The photographer and his team had only two hours available that afternoon, from 1 o'clock until the public were re-admitted at 3. In the middle of a long exposure one of the frosted glass filters which masked one of the two electric lamps shattered, and Pia had to call it off. He tried again on the evening of the 28th, beginning his precarious task at 9.30. This time everything went well. By 10.45 the platform had been laboriously trundled into position, the dynamos were doing their stuff. It was at 11 o'clock that night that Pia finally removed the cap which covered his Voigtländer lens and gave the Shroud a fourteen minute exposure. Then he gave it a second exposure of twenty minutes.

Pia's glass plates measured 51 by 63 centimetres, and are preserved in the Museum of the Holy Shroud at Via San Domenico 28 in Turin. He took them home post-haste, leaving his assistants to clear up the Cathedral, and when he developed the first of them he nearly jumped out of his skin: in fact he records that he almost let the plate drop in his astonished excitement. For under his very eyes had formed something new and totally unsuspected, a commanding face of calm and majestic beauty which none of the millions of devoted worshippers in the past had ever seen before. Indeed one of the staggering facts about the Shroud is that although to our certain knowledge it has been venerated as a sacred relic since the fourteenth century, the face which we now see reproduced on the cover of this book (and which is so hauntingly familiar to many of us) was not seen until the small hours of 29, May 1898, just over eighty years ago – in fact within living memory.

The explanation is in one sense simple, in another sense baffling. It seems that what meets the naked eye in looking at the Shroud is very like a photographic negative, which, when photographed, becomes positive in the negative of the photograph, when the *scuro* turns *chiaro* and the *chiaro, scuro*. The striking face which Pia first saw in 1898 is the positive preserved for centuries in the arcane negative of the Turin Shroud, which awaited the nineteenth-century invention of photography to reveal it.

People who maintain that the image on the Shroud is a medieval fake argue that what has happened here is the well-attested process known in the art world as 'reversal'. In a letter to the *Observer* of 9, April 1978, for instance, Mr John Parker (echoing the *Catholic Encyclopaedia* of 1912) claimed that 'the yellow colouring that represented the sweat of Christ has darkened to brown, through exposure to light and heat, thus converting the pristine "lights" to present "shades" and producing the accidental "negative photo" effects.' This solution might be plausible enough if the image of the Shroud-Man had been painted, but I repeat that scientists have detected no trace of any pigment on the Shroud.

By modern standards, Pia's historic photograph was not outstandingly brilliant, and a much better set was taken by a professional photographer called Giuseppe Enrie when the Shroud was exposed for twenty days in May 1931. Enrie took twelve photographs in all, and enjoyed every assistance from the Cardinal Archbishop, Monsignor Maurilio Fossati. Pia had had to contend with the thick plate-glass screen which the Principessa Clotilde had insisted should stand between relic and public in 1898; Enrie had no such obstacle, and his results were of a high degree of technical excellence: in fact it is his photographs that have become the prime evidence of sindonologists for more than forty years.

Since 1931 a further set of official photographs (in colour, in Wood's light, and in black-and-white) was taken in June 1969 by Giovanni Battista Judica-Cordiglia, and several unofficial snaps by people invited to the 1973 television exposition. But it was Pia's negative in 1898 that caused the sensation, for when it was published it met with a double hail of delight and protest. By the turn of the century the overwhelming weight of informed Catholic opinion, lay and clerical – particularly clerical – was against the authenticity of the Shroud. Pia was even accused of having cooked his evidence, and the suspicion that he might have touched up his plate lingered on until 1931, when Enrie took *his* photographs before about a hundred witnesses (one of whom, it is pleasant to record, was Secondo Pia himself, then 76).

Since the Enlightenment of the eighteenth century, the Roman Catholic Church has tended to be rather cautious about claims to the paranormal and supernatural outside the sacramental channel of Grace, and has taken a rigorous line with such alleged incursions of the noumenal as the appearances at La Salette and the miracles at Lourdes. Even Padre Pio, who during his lifetime was believed to bear Christ's stigmata, was never brought to Rome and lionised but left in a remote village of the Gargano.

Two of the most eminent opponents of the Shroud in the decade after the revealing negative of 1898 were a French Canon and an English Jesuit. Ulisse Chevalier (1841-1923) was a distinguished clerical scholar – in fact he was probably the most meticulous medievalist that France has ever produced. In 1899, 1900, 1902, and again in 1903 he threw the whole weight of his immense reputation for erudition into disproving the authenticity of the Shroud, and at least his *Étude critique sur l'origine du St Suaire de Lirey-Chambéry-Turin* (Paris, 1900) should be read and pondered by any serious inquirer today before he leaps to a facile conclusion. At much the same time Father Herbert Thurston, S.J. (1856-1939), weighed in at a more popular level of scholarship and voiced the rational disbelief of many Catholic and most Protestant historians in Britain. He concluded his influential essay of 1903 entitled *The Holy Shroud and the Verdict of History* with these confident words: 'The case [against the Shroud's authenticity] is here so strong that [. . .] the probability of an error in the verdict of history must be accounted, it seems to me, as almost infinitesimal.'

The irony of those opening years of this century was that some of the top intellectual brass of the Catholic Establishment outside Italy opposed the authenticity of the Shroud, while some of the most distinguished lay agnostic scientists were openly championing it. On 21, April 1902, for instance, Yves Delage (1854-1920), a very eminent Professor of Comparative Anatomy at the Sorbonne, who was known for his uncompromising stand against supernaturalism, gave a lecture on the Shroud before the Académie Française in which he declared his belief in its authenticity (and jeopardised his career in so doing). In the same year came out the careful scientific study entitled *Le Linceul du Christ* by Paul Vignon (1865-c1940), also of the Sorbonne, but later Professor of Biology at the Institut Catholique (Paris) and one of the Shroud's most convinced and able apologists of this century.

The fact that Delage and Vignon were scientists while Chevalier and Thurston were historians leads me to the conclusion that the evidence for the Shroud's authenticity is as scientifically strong as it is historically weak. The medical and scientific evidence is discussed in Chapters Three and Four of this book. The evidence from history is problematical to the nth degree. The most glaring (and many would say fatal) flaw in the claim of those who argue that this linen cloth was the actual shroud in which the crucified body of Jesus Christ was wrapped is the admitted fact that it boasts no authenticated history between the crucifixion and the fourteenth century. In other words, for more than the first two-thirds of its alleged existence it is attested by no certain record.

Furthermore, when the Shroud first comes to light, it appears in highly equivocal circumstances, to say the least, and halfway through a century which was notorious for devout chicanery and pious relic-mongering. For traditionally its history has been traced no further back than 1353, the year (most ominously) in which Giovanni Boccaccio finished writing his *Decameron* and King Edward III of England enacted the Statute of Præmunire, while King John II – nicknamed the Good – ruled in France. In that year it is said to have been lent to the new collegiate church of Lirey in Champagne, a little village about twelve miles from Troyes in France, by a French knight called Geoffroi de Charny who later fell at Poitiers on 19, September 1356.

Before the fourteenth century was out, this late arrival on the scene had acquired the two most dangerous – and seemingly best informed – opponents in its entire history. Both were Bishops, and both appear to have been men of exceptional probity in their generation. It is quite possible that the Shroud was not exposed at Lirey in Geoffroi's lifetime, but it is difficult to unravel the circumstances of its public debut with any accuracy. What seems reasonably certain is that within a year of Geoffroi's death the Bishop of Troyes, Henri de Poitiers, was already condemning the cult of this 'false' relic; and late in the year 1389 one of his successors in the see, Pierre d'Arcis, drew up a comprehensive memorandum for the Avignon Antipope Clement VII in which he claimed that the Shroud, far from being authentic, was the work of an artist who had confessed to the fraud. Here, in Herbert Thurston's translation, is the most damning passage from this forthright document, with the original Latin of some of the key sentences in parentheses:

The case, Holy Father, stands thus. Some time since in

this diocese of Troyes the Dean of a certain collegiate church, to wit, that of Lirey, falsely and deceitfully, being consumed with the passion of avarice, and not from any motive of devotion but only of gain, procured for his church a certain cloth cunningly painted, upon which by a clever sleight of hand was depicted the twofold image of one man, that is to say, the back and front, he falsely declaring and pretending that this was the actual shroud in which our Saviour Jesus Christ was enfolded in the tomb, and upon which the whole likeness of the Saviour had remained thus impressed together with the wounds which He bore [*quemdam pannum artificiose depictum in sua ecclesia procuravit habere, in quo subtili modo depicta erat duplex effigies unius hominis, videlicet tam a parte anteriori quam posteriori, falso asserens et confingens illud esse proprium Sudarium quo Salvator noster Jhesus Xpistus in sepulcro fuerat involutus, et in quo effigies tota ipsius Salvatoris, cum vulneribus que pertulit, remanserat sic impressa*]. This story was put about not only in the kingdom of France, but, so to speak, throughout the world, so that from all parts people came together to view it. And further to attract the multitude so that money cunningly be wrung from them, pretended miracles were worked, certain men being hired to represent themselves as healed at the moment of the exhibition of the shroud, which all believed to be the shroud of our Lord [*quod Domini Sudarium ab omnibus credebatur*]. The Lord Henry of Poitiers, of pious memory, then Bishop of Troyes, becoming aware of this, and urged by many prudent persons to take action, as indeed was his duty in the exercise of his ordinary jurisdiction, set himself earnestly to work to fathom the truth of this matter. For many theologians and other wise persons declared that this could not be the real shroud of our Lord having the Saviour's likeness thus imprinted upon it, since the holy Gospel made no mention of any such imprint, while, if it had been true, it was quite unlikely that the holy Evangelists would have omitted to record it, or that the fact should have remained hidden until the present time. Eventually, after diligent inquiry and examination, he discovered the fraud and how the said cloth had been cunningly painted, the truth being attested by the artist who had painted it, to wit, that it was a work of human skill and not miraculously wrought or bestowed [*Et tandem, solerti diligencia precedente et informacione super hoc facta,*

finaliter reperit fraudem   et quomodo pannus ille artificialiter
depictus fuerat, et probatum fuit eciam per artificem qui
illum depinxerat, ipsum humano ope factum, non miraculose
confectum vel concessum].[1]

And that, we might suppose, would be the end of that – the pretended relic had been dealt its *coup-de-grâce* by two men in the know. Their indictment seems overwhelming: a late start, bogus cures, a cunning fraud – we are in the century of Boccaccio's Frate Cipolla with a vengeance, in the very generation of Chaucer's Pardoner, who

> hadde a croys of latoun, ful of stones,
> And in a glas he hadde pigges bones.

For its own credibility's sake, the Shroud could hardly have surfaced at a worse time in the history of Latin Christendom. Overstatement is a perennial human pitfall, and few of us are not guilty of exaggeration in presenting a case in which we passionately believe. The temptation to gild the Catholic lily, to fortify the faith of the faithful by manipulating the evidence, to improve on the witness of history in the best of all possible causes, was perhaps never so strong as halfway through the fourteenth century. If the sermon's appeal to the ear could be clinched by a visual aid, and that aid was not to hand, then it must be manufactured for the salvation of immortal souls. But what began with good intentions ended as a money-making racket, for relic-mongering was (and still is) a profitable industry.

Pious frauds and cunning fakes abounded in the Age of Faith, from the Donation of Constantine to the marketing of Indulgences, and in general they obeyed the law of supply and demand. No doubt many genuine antiquities were brought back by pilgrims and crusaders from the Middle East, but many more were fabricated at home. Medieval imagination was inexhaustibly inventive, and ranged over the whole course of sacred history. On the principle of *what once was, must still be,* Scripture was combed for hints of detachable bits and pieces: a rung of Jacob's ladder, Jesse's root, the stone which the builders rejected and a feather from St Michael's wing – all were duly found and devoutly venerated. Relics proliferated in every shape and size. Between 1291 and 1295 the Holy House in which Jesus was brought up was borne through

1. Latin text in appendix to Chevalier, *Étude critique,* pp. VII-XII; English translation in Thurston, 'The Holy Shroud and the Verdict of History' in *The Month,* CI (January 1903), pp. 17-29 [reprinted in appendix to Ian Wilson, *The Turin Shroud* (London, 1978), pp. 230-235].

the air by angels in successive intercontinental flights from Nazareth to Loreto, where it is treasured to this day. The very year before the Reformation broke out, the skull of St Anne (the Virgin's mother) turned up in Berne as a nine days wonder until it was found that her earthly remains were preserved entire at Lyons. Blessed Mary's milk is still cherished in no fewer than eight churches, while relics of the life and death of Christ are legion: his swaddling clothes, a ray from the star of Bethlehem, the tears he shed at the tomb of Lazarus – even the evidence of Luke 2.21 came to light in due time. As late as 1844 his seamless coat was exhibited at Trier, and fragments of the True Cross which are still prized in holy places would furnish a choir with stalls. What could be more natural than that the True Shroud of Jesus should also be displayed in some village church in the reign of John the Good, appearing out of the blue like Melchizedek in the Book of Genesis?

But the linen cloth exposed at Lirey was by no means the only *Sudarium Domini* on show in France, nor was it the first. Chevalier has listed many of the rival shrouds of Jesus which have been preserved at one time or another in Christendom, some with his image imprinted on them, others without. (Readers of Dante will recall the *Santo Volto* adored in Lucca, and readers of Petrarch the *Veronica* venerated in Rome.) Reason tells us that they cannot all have been authentic, and common sense suggests that if one is false, all may be false. Is the Holy Shroud of Lirey-Chambéry-Turin just another pious fraud?

(If, in this discussion, I use the words 'fake' or 'forgery' or 'fraud' as an alternative to the authenticity of the Shroud, I do so because these are the charges which have been brought against it by its opponents since 1389. But such words only have meaning if there was an intention to deceive. A third alternative exists: might not the Shroud-Man, like *le Beau Dieu d'Amiens*, have been intended as representational religious art, which was later mistaken for reality because it was so realistic? Art is Art because it is not Nature: nobody after all would dream of calling the crucified Christ in Duccio's *Maestà* a fake.)

Let us suppose that the carbon 14 test, if and when it is applied to the Shroud, comes up with a fourteenth century date. What then? Most of us, I imagine, would dismiss the whole thing from our minds and rue the waste of time spent in studying it. But the niggle would probably remain in more than one conscience, because the scientific evidence of authenticity in fields other than that of carbon dating appears to be so strong. Could a *medieval*

Shroud of Christ be in any sense authentic? Even today, when the question of dating still hangs in the balance, some very curious arguments are employed to suggest that a fourteenth-century Shroud, if it proved beyond the competence of man to fabricate, could be the creation of God or the Devil. Let us briefly consider these possibilities in turn.

First, God. If the Shroud as we know it is not the result of natural processes but of supernatural intervention, then God could have produced this 'relic' by his divine power at any point in history, complete to the last authentic detail: why not halfway through the fourteenth century, just after the apocalyptic visitation of the Black Death, which between 1347 and 1349 carried off one third of the inhabitants of Christendom? As a token of his steadfast love and faithfulness, like the rainbow in the sky after Noah's Flood? This recalls the *omphalos* argument of Philip Gosse that the world was created *ex nihilo* six thousand years ago with all the evidences of its pre-history (symbolised by Adam's navel) and evolution implanted in it. But few people today are likely to be convinced by this line of reasoning. God *could,* but *would* not and remain God.

Secondly, the Devil. I have heard pious Protestants express the view that the Shroud was contrived by occult powers (probably among the Knights Templar) to occupy men's minds with a dead Christ instead of a risen and glorified Saviour. This echoes the Reformation argument of Bernardino Ochino in his *Tragoedie* of 1549 that the Roman Catholic Church was Satan's counterfeit of the true Church of Christ: why not the Shroud-Man as a diabolical counterfeit of the Body of Christ? But this contention is equally extreme. We know that the Devil can transform himself into an angel of light, but *could* he or *would* he have portrayed from painful memory that compelling face on the Turin Shroud?

We are left with no viable alternative: if the Shroud-Man is not the self-signature of Christ, then it must be the work of human ingenuity, with either good or evil intent. And yet, strangely enough, the more we examine this third hypothesis – which at first sight seems so much more rational than the direct intervention of God or Devil – the more it proves the most difficult of them all to swallow. Let us spare a thought at this point for the anonymous artist of genius: who was he? What craftsman during the reign of the first two Valois Kings had the requisite skills to create so exact a representation of the naked human body? Girard d'Orléans? Jean Coste? Jean Petit called Jean de Troyes? What we know of their work would hardly suggest that any of these leading painters at the court of King John II conceived and executed the portrait of Jesus on the Turin Shroud.

In the past, learned historians both clerical and lay have been satisfied that this portrait was *subtili modo depicta* and have championed the fake hypothesis. But what is so special about this relic that, six centuries after Bishop Henri de Poitiers unmasked it for a fraud, both Catholics and Protestants, Jews and Muslims, rationalists, nothingarians, scientists and even Oxbridge dons are busy discussing it this year, and most of them (as far as I can tell) are admitting that there is more in it than meets the eye? If I had to answer in one word, I should choose the Italian polysyllable which is in the mouth of so many sindonologists today: *i n f a l s i f i c a b i l e*. The more we investigate this fabulous sheet and the ghostly image it bears, the more we doubt whether any fourteenth-century artist could possibly have faked it. The Shroud-Man appears to be intrinsically unfakeable.

Let us enumerate some of the difficulties which beset the fake hypothesis. First, as we have seen, the admixture of cotton with the linen of the Shroud seems to preclude a European provenance for its fabric, and Dr Max Frei has found that some of the pollen clinging to it came from Asia Minor and the Middle East. But this in itself is not an insuperable difficulty, because a dedicated deceiver might have used a length of cloth brought back by some crusader, or could conceivably have sought the material for his hoax in Palestine himself – although such a quest would appear to be a trifle over-sophisticated for his day and age.

Secondly, and much more problematically, how on earth did the fourteenth-century faker project the image of the Shroud-Man on to the cloth? Monsieur le Truqueur *painted* it on, stated Bishop Pierre d'Arcis in his memorandum of 1389, and that sounds commonsensical enough until we remember that there are no brush-strokes visible on the Shroud, and no vestige of paint or any other known pigment. Another suggestion (by Dr Joseph Blinzler) is that the hoaxer made a life-size statue of a man and pressed it between the upper and nether halves of the folded linen sheet. But this proposed solution bristles with every sort of difficulty. In the first place, is there any record or tradition of sculpture to this degree of stark anatomical realism in mid-fourteenth-century France? (The first Lirey expositions of the Shroud occurred one generation before the birth of Brunelleschi and Donatello in Florence.) In the second place, the mere act of pressing alone, without pigment applied to the statue, would not have left any image on the cloth; and, in the third place, even if it had, it would have produced an image not perfect in proportion but distorted by physical contact, as anyone can confirm by the simple experiment of blacking his face with burnt cork and then pressing his handkerchief all over it. The basic fact remains: we just do not know by what natural means such an image could have been impressed upon the Shroud.

Thirdly, we have to account for the mysterious business of the photographic-type negative. We have already seen that it cannot be explained by 'reversal' because there is no paint on the Shroud. Yet there must be some natural explanation if the relic is a man-made fake. It would be an unusually clairvoyant and altruistic scoundrel who would perpetrate a hoax so subtle that none of his own generation, nor his children, nor children's children down to the tenth generation could appreciate it with their naked eyes, but which depended for its full impact and effect on the invention of photography five hundred years later.

But perhaps the most staggering clue to the genius of this hypothetical artist is that he has depicted Jesus with the nail-wound in his *wrist*. In France, Italy, Spain and elsewhere I have studied hundreds of paintings, sculptures and carvings of Christ's crucifixion and deposition from the thirteenth to the sixteenth centuries, and not one of them shows the nail-wound anywhere but in the palm of his hand. It is not until we come to Van Dyck in the seventeenth century that we find the first representation of Christ with the nail-wound through the wrist. His painting hangs in the Palazzo Reale in Genoa, a city in which he lived for some time, and it is possible that he may have been influenced in this detail by seeing the Shroud in passing through Turin.

Why did our fourteenth-century faker, against all the cultural conditioning of his times, place the nail-wound not in the palm but in the wrist? Anatomy and archaeology have since proved that he was perfectly correct. Dr Pierre Barbet, chief surgeon at the Paris hospital of St Joseph in the 1930s, conducted some revealing if macabre experiments with corpses and amputated limbs at that time. He established the fact that the weight of a human body would cause the nail to tear the flesh right up between the fingers if driven through the palm, because no bone would bar its way; whereas wrist-nailing ensured that the body stayed pinned to the *patibulum* of the cross when it was hoisted on to the *stipes*, which was already impaled in the ground at the place of execution.

It is surely no dishonour to medieval artists that they did not know this gruesome detail, for only in recent times have archaeologists, historians and medical men begun to re-discover the horrific techniques employed in crucifixion – once all too well known in the Roman Empire, but mercifully forgotten after Constantine abolished this form of capital punishment in 315 AD. Knowledge of the precise physical pains which Christ suffered had been lost long before any medieval artist began to depict them. The Gospels say his hands were nailed, so painters and sculptors naturally represented the wound in the palm. How then did the fourteenth-century faker, who lived a thousand years after the abolition of crucifixion, know this telling and authentic detail of wrist-nailing?

For authentic it was proved to be just over ten years ago, when the first known remains of a victim of crucifixion came to light in the outskirts of Jerusalem – a man in his mid-twenties called Jehohanan. His heel-bones were transfixed by a single nail and he had suffered the usual *crurifragium*. Although the nails were missing from his wrists, they had left on the radial bone their tell-tale marks of scratching and levigation.

And now for the most amazing detail of them all, which makes the fake hypothesis virtually incredible: if a nail pierces the wrist between radius and ulna, it touches the median nerve, which automatically causes the thumb to flex across the palm, so that it is invisible to anyone looking at the back of the hand. On the Turin Shroud we see the back of both the hands of Jesus Christ, but there is no sign of either thumb.

Authenticity is stamped all over this enigmatic relic, which just goes on springing surprise after surprise at its mysterious perfection from year to year. The impressive matching of the scourge-marks with the pattern of two soldiers administering the flogging, one either side, one taller than the other: the angle of the blood-flows on the forearm, mathematically exact for crucifixion: the dimensions of the side-wound, and its emission of both blood and water: the stupendous witness of the wounds (in total verisimilitude) caused by the spiky cap: all these features of the Shroud-Man and many more compel us to admit the harmonious integrity of this unfakeable image. But it is above all the face which rivets our responsive gaze – 'an appearance so marred beyond human semblance, a man of sorrows and acquainted with grief' (Isaiah 52.14, 53.3) – yet a face of tranquil dignity, of royal authority, of divine beauty – a countenance in a million million: unique. If the Shroud-Man looked like this in death, how did he appear in life?

Toi, qui-es-tu? – asked Paul Claudel, brought face to face with the Turin Shroud and its haunting image. The answer is unavoidable: it is Jesus Christ our Lord. In the astonished words of the centurion who saw him die: 'Truly this man was the Son of God!' (Mark 15.39.)

If then this relic is the authentic Shroud of Christ and bears his imperishable imprint, where was it between about 30 AD and 1353? The short and truthful answer is that we simply do not know. It was evidently not displayed publicly in its present form, for if it had been there would surely exist some record of its display. It is not impossible that it remained hidden for a millennium in some remote monastic fastness, like Codex Sinaiticus before it was discovered by Tischendorf: but this we cannot tell.

Of course there have been many clever reconstructions of its missing history, the most recent and ingenious being the suggestion made by Mr Ian Wilson that the Turin Shroud and the Edessa Mandylion are one and the same thing.[2] 'Mandylion' is a Greek word which means head-shawl or kerchief, and was applied to a piece of ancient cloth which was venerated in Asia Minor (first at Edessa and later at Constantinople) until it vanished without trace in 1204 AD. It was said to bear the image of the bearded face of Christ, a likeness *acheiropoietos,* or 'not made by hand'.

Mr Wilson argues that the Mandylion was the Shroud of Christ so folded up and protected by ornamental trellis that only the image of the face was displayed. His hypothesis, presented with a wealth of circumstantial evidence, is as attractive as it is unconvincing; for, although it would have explained so much, it is fraught with difficulties which many critical readers will find insuperable. One is purely practical, and might occur to any housewife. If a linen sheet is folded and protected so that only a small part of it is exposed to the air, after several centuries that part is likely to have suffered discoloration. If the Shroud spent more than half its life as the Mandylion, there should be a circular area around the face of Christ which is more yellowed than the rest of the cloth: but this is not the case.

2. *The Turin Shroud* (London, 1978), pp. 91-165. See also his articles 'Tomb to Turin' in *The Ampleforth Journal,* vol. LXXXIII Part 1 (Spring 1978), pp. 9-23, and 'Mystery of the Shroud' in *The Sunday Times* colour supplement 26 March 1978. Even if they do not agree with Mr Wilson's central thesis, all English-speaking sindonologists will value his writings for their clarity of presentation and abundance of accurate detail.

How did the Shroud come into the hands of Geoffroi de Charny? His son said it was *liberaliter oblatam,* or a grace and favour gift, and his granddaughter, Margaret de Charny, widow of Humbert de Villersexel, Comte de la Roche, (who in 1418 removed the relic from Lirey and in 1453 gave it to Duke Louis of Savoy) claimed in 1443 that her grandfather had acquired the Shroud in war (*bello partum*). Both statements suggest that it was the legitimate spoil of battle, the reward for taking part in a crusade. Some historians have concluded – on insufficient evidence – that it was given to Geoffroi de Charny by the dying King Philip VI.[3]

Most sindonologists trace a connection between Lirey and Constantinople via the crusades, and some would extend the Shroud's itinerary to include Acre and Cyprus.[4] Bishop Langton Fox and others before him have pointed to a shroud which was preserved in Besançon Cathedral until it disappeared during a fire in 1349, and have suggested an identification with the Shroud of Lirey.[5] Here again we must confess we do not know. Any statements made about the relic's travels or condition before it appeared at Lirey in the 1350s are in the realm of speculation and not of recorded history. On circumstantial evidence Mr Wilson has made out an interesting case for his argument that after 1204 the Mandylion-Shroud was in the hands of the Knights Templar (and was in fact the 'idol' which they were accused of worshipping) until their suppression in 1307, passing from this Order to Geoffroi de Charny; but his advocacy is marred by special pleading, and at times his conclusions do not appear to follow from his premises.[6]

If the Shroud is authentic, do we need its history before 1353 to prove it? As historians we are programmed to answer Yes: any artefact which turns up in one century purporting to come from another is rightly an object of suspicion until proved genuine,

3. One of the most interesting accounts of the pre-1353 'history' of the Shroud is given by Fr Paul de Gail, S. J., in his *Histoire religieuse du Linceul du Christ* (Paris, 1974).

4. For a sixteenth-century account of the Shroud by an Archbishop of Bologna, see Alfonso Paleotti's *Esplicatione del sacro Lenzuolo ove fu involto il Signore* (Bologna, 1598 & 1599).

5. 'One cannot help surmizing that it was given to the king [Philip VI] by someone who had looted it from Besançon', Langton Fox, *The Holy Shroud* (London, 1978), p. 6 (Catholic Truth Society pamphlet).

6. As for instance when he claims: 'Upon such speculation the most challenging clue of all emerges – that it was the Templars who had the Shroud, and that it was in the family of one of the masters of the order that it found its new home', *The Turin Shroud*, p. 164.

whether it is Drake's plaque, the Vinland map, or Piltdown Man. But as logicians we are bound to answer No: authenticity is authenticity, and *a priori* we can argue that if an article is genuine it is genuine, whether we have history to prove it or not. If I find a Rembrandt in my attic its authenticity is not altered by the fact that I cannot account for its provenance. A pot, a coin, or a statue can lie buried for two millennia and retain their integrity: they are what they are. When I was in St Andrews last January, the Professor of Ecclesiastical History took me round St Mary's College, and showed me a black leather chalice-holder embossed with the insignia of the Virgin Mary and inscribed with Latin tags. He told me that it was found last year in a college cupboard, where it had gathered dust unnoticed since before the Reformation. Improbable, but true.

The Shroud is such a remarkable thing that, in the last analysis, there can be only two honest opinions about it. The first (which occurs most readily to the Protestant and rationalist in me) is that it is a piece of fourteenth-century representational art, and therefore probably a fake – an unusual fake, admittedly, well-intentioned possibly, ingenious certainly, but *not* the shroud in which the body of Jesus Christ was wrapped; or, if indeed the length of linen was that shroud, then the image on it has been added later by human hand as a pious fraud, by some process which even modern scientists do not understand. And of course if the image is not authentic, then the veneration of it comes perilously close to breaking the First and Second Commandments.

The alternative opinion is almost too shattering to the equanimity of most of us to entertain for more than a moment or two. It is that in the Turin Shroud we have not only the linen cloth in which the body of the Lord Jesus was wrapped, but also a representation of that body portrayed by other than human hands, by some supernatural process which confounds all explanation. Either way the thing is a marvel – of illusion if it is a fake, or of reality if it is not. But it is my conviction that in this most mysterious thing – embarrassing in its uniqueness, exciting in its challenge – we face the same reality that confronts us in the Incarnation and Resurrection of Christ. In both those central miracles of world history was manifested the splendour of God: could it be that the radiant incandescence of that almighty act of love and power when the Son of God 'was raised by the glory of the Father' has scorched his image and likeness on the Shroud, a sign for our scientific century which demands scientific proof?

As a Christian I must declare my belief that the truth of Christianity does not require such signs as the Turin Shroud, for its proof is the living witness of the Spirit of God in all who receive Jesus Christ as Saviour, Lord and God; but perhaps from time to time we fallible human beings need such demonstrations of a reality which transcends our powers of explanation to jolt us out of the complacency of our agnosticism and confirm our faltering faith. Lord, I believe: help thou mine unbelief!

Chapter Two

Bringing the Shroud to the test
David Sox

The present day owner of the Turin Shroud is Umberto II, the last King of Italy, now living in exile in Cascais, Portugal. The son of Victor Emmanuel III and Elena Petrovitch of Montenegro was King for thirty four days. He left Italy in 1946 after losing a referendum on the monarchy by a small margin. In this democratic way, the once powerful Savoyard family which had ruled for so long, came to an end. Now separated from his wife, Marie José of the Belgian royal family, Umberto makes his home in Villa Italia, a large but unpretentious house directly across from an abyss in the sea called the Boca do Inferno (the Mouth of Hell). All his children, including his heir, Victor Emmanuel IV, have been disappointments to the ex-King. The prince has no interest in the Savoyard patrimony. Friends close to the ex-King think he may designate the patronage of the dynasty to the cadet line in the person of the Duke of Aosta, Amadeo, who is married to the daughter of the Count of Paris.

All of this vitally concerns the future of the Turin Shroud. The Republic of Italy has been confiscating the Savoyard property in a slow but determined manner since ex-King Umberto left his homeland and he has said privately that he plans to give his family's most prized possession, the Shroud, to the Vatican at his death. He has always had an interest in the Cloth and, unlike his wife who dismissed it as spurious in a caustic footnote in her unpublished Savoyard history, has always felt that it was genuine. When he left Italy, he told the Archbishop of Turin that he would have to be the custodian of the relic for him and that has remained the practical arrangement ever since. In theory, the ex-King can do anything he desires with the Shroud; in practice, however, the Archbishop's word has been the deciding factor. The heads of the Archdiocese of Turin have always sought the ex-King's permission, plus that of the Pope, concerning questions about the Shroud. The ex-King has made it clear that any investigations concerning the relic would have their impetus from the Archbishop.

Until fairly recently, the fact of Savoyard ownership was used

41

as a delaying tactic in answering pressure for scientific testing of the Shroud. That excuse can no longer be used, since ex-King Umberto has stated again recently that he has no objection to letting competent research go as far as it can in exploring the mysteries of the image on the Cloth. At the beginning of his exile, he inherited his father's feeling that, since the 1889 and 1931 photographings had produced such astounding evidence, it was not necessary to have scientific testing of the Shroud. If observers would not be satisfied with what photography has presented, they probably would not be convinced with the results of any scientific tests set before them. However, in the past few years, ex-King Umberto has become convinced that further testing of the Shroud should be allowed.

The Roman Catholic Church has never promulgated any doctrines concerning the Shroud. By their very nature, relics were important only in terms of the holy person to whom they were attached. Unless suspicions were aroused concerning a particular relic the Church has refrained from declaring any of its vast accumulation of relics authentic or unauthentic. The Holy Shroud of Turin has been surrounded by great veneration in the past. Several Popes have shown interest in the Cloth, but this has always been a personal matter. Four days before his death on 10, February 1939, Pope Pius XI received a group of school children in what was to be the last audience of his life. Holding a copy of the Shroud face, he explained to them that this was the face of the Redeemer. In more recent years, Pope John XXIII was said to have exclaimed: 'This can only be the Lord's doing' when he was given a copy of the image. During the televised 'act of veneration' of the Shroud (22-23, November 1973) Pope Paul VI described the 'deep impression' it had made on him when he first saw it in 1931.

It is no secret that Pope Paul has been responsible for breaking down some of the resistance in Turin to the testing of the Cloth. Before his reign, all research concerning the relic had been done using only photographs of the image. Repeated pleas from Shroud enthusiasts all over the world for an exposition and direct testing fell on deaf ears until the secret investigations of 1969 and 1973, and the televised exposition of 1973. It is difficult to fathom the attitude of Turin towards its palladium. Some have pointed to a certain jealously on the part of the Turin clergy. There has always been a strong sense of independence among the Piedmontese and a native conceit. Of all the areas of Italy, Piedmont was the only one which managed to remain free of foreign domination. It was natural that this section would be the leading one in the movement for national independence and unity in the nineteenth century.

After the impressive photographing by Giuseppe Enrie in 1931, and with the interest of such men as Barbet, Delage and Vignon, the study of the Shroud became a science known as Sindonology, and two Sindonological Congresses were held in 1939 and 1950. These meetings covered almost every conceivable aspect of the Cloth's study and the participants presented resolutions for direct testing of the Shroud. Despite this, and unremitting pressure from Father Rinaldi's Holy Shroud Guild in the United States, nothing happened until 1969, and it would not be until 1976 that anyone outside the small circle of 'experts' appointed by the Archbishop of Turin would know who and what was involved in the secret tests. How these tests came about gives one an understanding of the difficulties to be faced in bringing the Turin Shroud to scientific research.

Cardinal Michele Pellegrino, Archbishop of Turin until October 1977, had the reputation of being a progressive in the post-Vatican II Church, but he was surrounded by a rather cautious group of clergy when it came to dealing with the Shroud. By his own admission he was never vitally concerned with the relic – his interests were with the considerable social problems of Turin – and so he appointed his Press Officer, Monsignor Jose Cottino, Overseer of Shroud Matters. Monsignor Cottino was an unfortunate choice in the eyes of many who dealt with him: one rarely got a direct answer from him. Although it was clear to some that there had been an investigation of sorts in 1969, Monsignor Cottino flatly denied that anything more than a routine assessment of the present day condition of the Cloth had been performed. So that they could 'complete their work' and 'not be involved in any debate', no names of the Archbishop's Commission of 'experts' would be released.

Cardinal Pellegrino felt that a televised exposition would avoid the problem of the traditional public expositions in the past – millions of tourists in Turin and a commercialisation of the event. On Friday, 23, November 1973, hanging upright in a massive but unadorned frame, with no protective glass, the Cloth was exposed to the strong lights of television. The programme was rather stilted and over-devotional, with scenes of the Cardinal praying in the middle of a line of altar boys. No explanation of the scientific aspects of the Shroud was mentioned and most viewers were probably more confused than spiritually enriched at the end of the presentation. Turin had won the day in making certain that no possible controversy would mar this act of veneration.

Only members of the Commission knew what was to happen the next day. Four nuns of the Daughters of St. Joseph carefully removed seventeen samples from the Shroud. They took two pieces – one 40mm x 13mm from the bottom right-hand edge and another 40mm x 10mm from the Shroud's side strip – three threads with no portion of the image, and twelve with clear portions of the image. Professor Gilbert Raes, a Belgian textile expert, would study the two pieces and two threads. Professors Frache, Mari and Rizzatti would analyse eleven threads for possible traces of blood and Professors Filogamo and Zina would conduct microscopic analysis on the two threads supplied to them.

It was an individual who has been known by three names, Hans Naber, Kurt Berna and John Reban, who first indicated to newsmen that he knew from 'an unnamed source' that there would be a private examination of the Turin Cloth. As a self-styled 'expert' and propagandist for the view that Jesus did not die on the Cross, Naber had waited for such a moment. He had a 'field day' with the Press: 'Vatican Accused of Secret Probe on Holy Shroud' and 'Christ's Holy Shroud May Be Destroyed'. He contended to newsmen that what was about to ensue was not an examination of the Cloth but a destruction of the evidence that Jesus was alive when he was removed from the Cross. What disturbed many was not Naber's wild claims and imaginings which the Press eventually discarded, but rather the way Turin reacted by playing right into his hands by saying nothing.

British medical expert on the Shroud, Dr David Willis, wrote in an article 'False Prophet and the Holy Shroud', published in *The Tablet* on 13, June 1970, ". . . the way things were actually carried out, and the lack of any proper information after nearly a year, have permitted him, without a shred of justification, to pillory both the Cardinal and the Vatican. This can all be corrected in the future by Cardinal Pellegrino resisting all temptations to secrecy and insisting on a full-scale, open, legally-attested, international, scientific investigation. An Italian team acting in secrecy will convince no one."

Rumours continued that some tests had been performed in 1969 and 1973. On 3, March 1976, the BBC Radio Four programme 'Sunday' gave the news that a Swiss pollen analyst, Dr Max Frei, had removed pollen from the Cloth when he was called to Turin to certify the photographs taken by Giovanni Battista Judica-Cordiglia in 1969. Dr Frei stated that he was 'able to verify that there were specks of pollen present from Constantinople . . .

and from plants known to have grown in Palestine some twenty centuries ago.'

One of those who felt that the whole affair had been handled badly was Shroud enthusiast Group Captain Leonard Cheshire V.C. In response to reporter Ted Harrison's question, ('What's gone wrong?'), he exclaimed, 'I am not unfair in saying that those who are interested in the Shroud the world over are bitterly disappointed with the way the authorities at Turin have handled the whole affair. They have conducted an investigation . . . but they kept quiet about what they were doing.'

It would not be until eight months later that the Cardinal would attempt to clarify what sort of examination had taken place. Despite the lamentable secrecy and the limitation of examiners to the area of Turin, the report made it clear that direct testing was the only future for Sindonology. While the general tone of the report was inconclusive as to authenticating the relic, Dr Frei's pollen analysis had indicated the possibility of pollen species from first-century Palestine, and perhaps more important was the observation that the image is completely superficial – it does not penetrate into the cloth. No grains of any impregnating material could be seen through the electron microscope on the samples removed for study. When the nuns were making extractions of thread from an area of a 'scourge-mark', one thread broke, and with the unaided eye it could be observed that the reddish tint of the image was only on the surface of the thread, while the inside filaments appeared to be perfectly white. The minute granules forming the image could be seen but not identified even with 50,000X magnification. The granules seemed neither to have seeped nor penetrated between the fibres and they were both insoluble and resistant to acetic acid.

By 1973 there were eleven official members of the Commission appointed by the Archbishop. All of them were Italian, except Professor Raes. This restriction meant that they would only be able to go 'so far' in their studies, because of the limitation of the scientific equipment at their disposal. Professor Silvio Curto, who is curator of Turin's impressive Egyptian Museum, noted that the fabric is not like the ancient Egyptian plain weaving; it is a 'twill', a herringbone pattern probably originating in Syria or Mesopotamia. Professor Raes of Ghent, who is acquainted with almost every conceivable ancient and modern fabric, asserted that in his opinion it was *possible* that the linen was of the time of Christ. He discovered the presence of cotton in the sample from the main body of the Shroud. The other sample was from the side strip which may or may not have been an integral part of the original Cloth.

The fibres he saw corresponded to the species *Gossypium Herbaceum,* which is the cotton of the Middle East. This added a certain interesting touch to the discovery of the fabric, in that cotton is not grown in Europe, and the Mishnah clearly allows the mixing of flax and cotton (not so with wool, which still is a transgression of the 'mixing of kinds' to Orthodox Jews.) Ironically the samples he studied provided more material than was necessary for carbon dating by newly improved methods, but this information was apparently unknown to the Commission members who opposed the test, assuming that it would require a handkerchief-size sample, as was the case with the original Libby test.

No haematic substance was discovered in tests for blood, performed by Professor Giorgio Frache, a Waldensian Protestant, of Modena University. Red blood cells contain a peroxidase which will turn blue when confronted with mixtures containing benzidine but because this did not occur with the ten threads containing 'blood' images, the assumption has been made that perhaps the original traces of blood have been rendered unidentifiable by the intense heat of the 1532 fire to which the Shroud was subjected in Chambéry, or perhaps this was due to the image-creation process. Neither Professor Frache's nor the tests performed by Professor Filogamo, blood-analysis specialist from the Department of Human Anatomy of Turin University, were able to identify the yellow-red granules that compose the blood images of the Shroud. One thing was certain: it was neither blood nor any fraudulent substance according to both reports. It was noted that the use of more powerful microscopes, such as the scanning electron or the ion microprobe, might furnish 'more significant data.' Unfortunately there seemed to be no access to them.

Professor Naomi Gabrielli, formerly of the Art Galleries of Piedmont, suggested that the Shroud was '. . . the work of a great artist of the late fifteenth century and early sixteenth century, who used the Leonardo technique of shading . . .'. It was Dr Frei's pollen analysis which attracted the most attention. He had obtained permission to remove 'dust' from the linen, which he said included pollen from Palestine, Turkey and central Europe. He was able to announce that the Palestinian samples were identical with pollen fossils from the Negev and the Jordan Valley of the time of Christ. This created great excitement in the European Press and only recently have archaeological researchers questioned such a precise identification as he made. The area around Jerusalem comprises such a rich variety of climate and environment that its flora changes greatly within short distances. Dr Frei's study will probably require new samples and further analysis.

The third photographer of the Shroud, Judica-Cordiglia, son of another Commission member, had the most modern equipment possible at his disposal and although the first-time colour photographs were quite satisfactory, the results of the black and white photographs were seen by some as inferior to those of Giuseppe Enrie in 1931.

Despite considerable limitations, it was evident that Cardinal Pellegrino's Commission had started a process which was now irreversible for the future study of the relic. The reliquary had been opened to direct scientific analysis which would ask more and more questions. As Father Rinaldi put it: 'Even if Turin botched this first positive step by limiting the work of the Commission and surrounding it with uncalled-for secrecy, it was a breakthrough of a sort.'

The Turin Commission was not aware that the two samples removed from the Shroud for Professor Raes' study could be used for carbon 14 dating. Improvements in both equipment and techniques by several North American laboratories had narrowed the required sample weight from approximately 40 grams in 1950, to about 60 milligrams in 1976. Even the smaller of the two samples removed was above this new range and several individuals interested in the test possibility in England and America were aware of this fact. During a visit to Turin in July 1976, I decided to find out where those samples were. With friends in England, I was convinced that the carbon dating test was the single most important trial for the relic, certainly the one most mentioned by those taking a scientific interest in the Shroud.

Monsignor Cottino, still acting as Cardinal Pellegrino's spokesman on matters related to the Shroud, was certain that the samples were back in the reliquary of the Royal Chapel in Turin Cathedral. Others said that they had been destroyed, but Professor Curto assured me they were still in Ghent with Professor Raes, and so they were. A letter from him confirmed the fact. Expressing an interest in the new carbon dating, he ended his correspondence with one sentence which whetted our hopes: 'I should like to know how to proceed for the forwarding of the samples.'

By chance, Dr Walter McCrone, a microanalyst from Chicago, who was interested in various tests with the Shroud including the carbon dating, was in London at the time of the correspondence. Dr McCrone is best known for his testing of Yale

University's Vinland Map, which, to the horror of Italo-Americans, might have indicated a pre-Columbian mapping of the New World. He discovered that, while the map's parchment was indeed medieval, the ink contained a synthesised pigment unknown until 1920.

Professor Raes produced the samples for Dr McCrone and me in his Ghent flat on 19, September 1976. They were kept in what looked like an old scrapbook for postage stamps. Dr McCrone was able to give them a preliminary investigation with his portable set of microscopes and other instruments and his initial reaction was that they were suitable for testing. Unknown to us, Professor Raes had been in touch with a carbon 14 specialist from the University of Louvain-La-Neuve, Professor D. Apers, who was interested in the new test possibility but not as proposed by Dr McCrone. The method Professor McCrone was suggesting at this time was using 'nuclear track emulsions' which Professor Apers stated bluntly was not acceptable to the carbon dating experts he knew.

Professor Raes became nervous over the fact that he still possessed such valuable samples. They had been in his care for three years and I had asked him during this meeting to get in contact with Turin over the possibility of a test. Members of the Commission reacted by asking for the samples to be returned, which he did – by post! They were then placed in the sacristy vault of the Royal Chapel where they were to stay.

When interviewed by *The Sunday Times* as part of a 'Spectrum' article 'Is this the face of Jesus?' published on 10, April 1977, Monsignor Pietro Caramello, the custodian of the Royal Chapel, said that no pieces were ever cut from the relic, 'and we exclude ever doing so'. In a letter to the editor, published the following Sunday, I not only gave the pages (79-83) and photograph references to these samples in the Turin Commission Report (over which Monsignor Caramello presided) but also indicated that I had seen them in Ghent and that the Shroud's legal owner, ex-King Umberto II, had expressed a keen interest in the possible testing when I had been with him in Portugal the previous week.

The next stimulus for investigating the Shroud's image came from a highly unlikely source – the United States military establishment. When Father Rinaldi and Father Otterbein of the Holy Shroud Guild returned to the United States after the 1973 television exposition, they were contacted by a young United States Air Force Captain and physicist, Doctor John Jackson, about an entirely new approach to the image formation that he and an equally youthful colleague, Doctor Eric Jumper, an Aerodynamics Professor, were making during their free time from classes at the Air Force Weapons Laboratory in Albuquerque, New Mexico. The two became great friends, and with a computer and image-processing specialist, Donald Devan, began to analyse the 1931 Enrie photographs of the Shroud with sophisticated computer equipment, including the VP-8 Analyser, which was used in the American space programme for reconstructing the relief of the moon's surface from photographs.

The analyser supplied some fascinating information: the Shroud not only has the properties of a photographic negative as was discovered in 1898, but it is three-dimensional in character, a quality unheard of in the history of art or photography. Ordinary photographs do not have this property – transformed into vertical relief they will present obvious distortions with noses pushed into faces and arms into chests. To obtain the '3-D' photographs we see on post cards and in special effects, at least two photographs placed at set angles have to be used. In the case of the Shroud, the resulting three-dimensional portrait presented a natural, proportioned body lacking any apparent distortion (photograph 7).

Ever since Secondo Pia's 1898 photographs, it had been noted that the image darkness on the Shroud varies from point to point, suggesting a creation process acting across a distance from the image. Paul Vignon, the leading Sindonologist of the early part of this century, spoke of the intensity varying inversely with cloth-body distance. To measure this possibility, Dr Jackson and Dr Jumper made a cloth model of the relic onto which they projected the Enrie photographs, marking the varied stains and body marks. Eleven cadets were tested to find a matching body type and the one who best corresponded was a 175 pound young man, whose height was 5' 10½" – almost exactly what anatomists had previously calculated from photographic studies. A microdensitometer was used to scan the ridge-line of the photographic reconstruction of the cloth-body distance. Mathematical correlation of the relationship between the image intensity and the degree to which the cloth was separated from the body at the various points. There was little doubt in their minds that the image creation process had acted over a distance, rather than by any direct contact method as had been suggested by some previous analysers. The two Doctors felt they had discovered strong arguments in favour of the Turin Shroud's authenticity: '. . . an artist living in the fourteenth century would not have been able to encode three-dimensional information by adjusting intensity levels in order to correspond everywhere to actual cloth-separations.' The study of the Turin Shroud had entered the space age!

Albuquerque, New Mexico, is surrounded by various military complexes, including Los Alamos, remembered for its atomic bomb experiments. In this unlikely environment the Shroud would receive thorough scrutiny. Dr Jackson and Dr Jumper with their new associates in research, and the Holy Shroud Guild, invited some forty Shroud experts from Europe and the United States to a two-day Conference on 23 and 24, March 1977 in an Albuquerque motel. The stated purpose of the event was to bring those attending up to date with what others were doing in research on the Shroud and to prepare a specific research proposal to the authorities in Turin.

Much of the discussion was highly technical and exploratory, with suggestions of such possibilities as digital enhancement of Shroud images, and considerations of molecular diffusion and radiation as the image formation process on the cloth. Some of the discussion had immediate application for future testing. Colour spectroscopic analysis indicated that what appears to be varied colorations on the Shroud (the body and blood images and the burn marks) all record the same intensity. The implications were that the total Shroud image has pronounced similarity to a scorching. None of the speakers went on record saying what they felt had caused the image, but it was apparent that only one possibility was being taken seriously by most of the scientists: a high-intensity, short-burst radiation of some sort. Dr Ray Rogers, archaeologist and thermochemist from Los Alamos, indicated that the computer image studies tended to rule out altogether the chance that the image was painted. No linear strokes were observed and there was no change of colour from dark to light tones.

It was apparent to all involved with the New Mexico Conference that studies had gone about as far as possible using information gleaned from photographs. It was also recognised that the Turin tests had raised questions which needed direct exploration. The possibilities of future tests and direct observations of the Shroud were so many and so varied that their proposals might have the opposite effect of what had happened in Turin – involving too many people and too varied a personnel. It was, of course, all conjecture; just how much would Turin be willing to accept? Carbon dating was put at the top of the list of proposals and Conference participant, Dr Walter McCrone, was viewed as the best-suited person to oversee this possibility. He has no carbon dating facility at his Chicago laboratory but he is in touch with all the centres perfecting the new C-14 test. What Dr McCrone does possess is two million dollars' worth of the most sophisticated microscopes and microprobes in the world. One of his prized instruments is the ion microprobe which is able to identify which of the 104 chemical elements are present in a particular sample. In view of the nature of the image as reported in the Turin Commission Report, this was viewed as a top priority.

Dr Ray Rogers stressed the importance of X-ray fluorescence. This test would be able to detect the presence of iron in the 'blood stains'; indeed, its use can indicate characteristically high concentrations of any trace elements. When bombarded with a primary beam of X-ray, an object's secondary X-rays (the fluorescence) will be emitted. This fluorescence will be determined by the elements present in the sample. By comparing the sample's fluorescence with standards based on emissions from known samples, the scientist can tell what elements are present and their approximate concentration. In the case of the Shroud, particular attention would be paid not only to iron, but also to phosphorus, indicating blood possibility, chlorine from sweat, silver from the burning reliquary casket in Chambéry and metals of a high atomic number which might display pigments not yet detected by other methods.

Two other forms of radiation which have been invaluable in authenticating art works, infra-red and ultra-violet, were also seen as essential analyses. Infra-red might indicate a hitherto unexamined image, and ultra-violet causes retouchings in paintings to fluoresce. New photographs tailored to be translated into number equivalents for further computer analysis were suggested. One square inch of film could be represented by a million separate points, each of which describe the relative darkness and light at a given point. The possibilities of this type of investigation are 'essentially infinite' according to one of the speakers, Dr. Donald Lynn, Image Enhancement specialist from the Jet Propulsion Laboratory, Pasadena, California. Textural differences at any point on the Shroud and the relative darkness of each image could be accurately measured.

There was little doubt at the New Mexico meeting that the Turin Commission had opened the door to a barrage of possible investigations. A comprehensive list of test proposals would be submitted to Turin, which meant that the Turin Shroud might be subjected to an investigation few art objects or historical artefacts had yet known. This indicated both the complexities of the mystery of the relic and the seriousness with which some had come to consider it in the 1970's.

Dr Jumper and Dr Jackson had succeeded in bringing the Shroud into a scientific arena only hinted at by previous discussions of Sindonologists. The next stimulus occurred in London in the autumn of 1977. British interest in the Turin Shroud had been scattered and disorganised compared with the American efforts. Individuals such as Group Captain Leonard Cheshire, V.C., Miss Vera Barclay and Dr David Willis had contributed valuable insights but little was accomplished in an organised fashion. The need for a broadly-based society was recognised in 1976 and gradually the British Society for the Turin Shroud came into being. With the interest of Anglican leaders, the Rt Revd Dr John A.T. Robinson and the Rt Revd Dr Hugh Montefiore, the group was to take on a fully ecumenical flavour at the outset. The inauguration of the society was at the 'Symposium on the Shroud of Turin' held at the Anglican Institute of Christian Studies on 16 and 17, September 1977.

Unlike the New Mexico Conference, the London Symposium was open to subscribers and those who attended came from surprisingly diverse backgrounds: Muslim, Jewish, Methodist, Eastern Orthodox, Anglican and Roman Catholic. The Shroud entered an ecumenical phase and Turin took special note. '*La Stampa*', the prestigious Turin-based newspaper, gave wide coverage to the event with such headlines as 'London Proposes: the Shroud Should Undergo New Tests'. Considerable fascination was shown in the non-Roman Catholic concern expressed and the fact that the Conference was in Britain. As '*La Stampa*' put it: '. . . undoubtedly an exceptional event in a country which, since its separation from the Papacy, has always shown a great deal of scepticism — if not downright hostility towards similar forms of cult'. With this momentum, a delegation led by Dr Jackson, Dr Jumper and Fr Rinaldi went to Turin to meet a new Commission to put forward the 'New Mexico proposals'.

It was hoped that the tests would take place in connection with the four hundredth celebration of the relic's presence in Turin the next year. The initial reaction was encouraging; the Turin spokesman seemed overwhelmed by the highly organised American team. Towards the end of the last session of talks, Monsignor Caramello, who had been the President of the 1969 Commission, felt there was nothing left to be done but draft letters of the proposals, including carbon dating, to the new Archbishop of Turin and ex-King Umberto.

Cardinal Pellegrino had announced his intention to resign for reasons of health months earlier. The Pope accepted this and named Anastasio Ballestrero, Bishop of Bari, as the new head of the Turin Archdiocese. The Bishop had not been in Turin at the time of the talks and when he did arrive his first episcopal act concerning the Shroud was to seek a wide consensus among his clergy and laity by circulating a questionnaire through ecclesiastical channels as to what should be done concerning the relic in 1978. When Fr Rinaldi and I saw him before Christmas, 1977, he gave both the physical and spiritual impression of Pope John XXIII. Dressed in the black cassock worn by any priest and greeting us with the kiss of peace, he listened attentively to our concerns that the tests be allowed. He was fascinated by the fact that non-Roman Catholics were interested in the Shroud and took careful note that ex-King Umberto had given his initial approval to the tests. It was also apparent that he would act cautiously, obviously desiring time to become better acquainted with the total situation.

While the Archbishop began quietly to assess the situation, two of the participants of the New Mexico Conference, Monsignor Giulio Ricci and his secretary, Miss Mary Elizabeth Patrizzi, made independent efforts to get the Shroud carbon dated. Monsignor Ricci has been archivist at the Vatican for the Congregation of Bishops and has had a long interest in the relic. He has made endless mathematical calculations of the dimensions of the Shroud's image and has developed a complicated theory as to how the linen wrapped the body. Probably no man alive knows more about each marking on the Cloth. The New Mexico meeting had given him and his secretary the impression that they should pursue 'diplomatic' overtures for the carbon test and they did. Their efforts were basically unknown to others who were trying to get the test proposals accepted.

On 21, September 1977, following the meeting in Turin, Monsignor Ricci, Miss Patrizzi and Dr McCrone met ex-King Umberto in Geneva to discuss the carbon dating test. A 'phone call by Miss Patrizzi to Monsignor Caramello in Turin ascertained that the samples were still in the sacristy safe, and Monsignor Ricci's secretary stated that the ex-King was authorising their release for testing. Monsignor Caramello wanted more than a 'phone call as assurance of the ex-King's desire, and when the implications of this attempt were realised in Turin a set-back to the possible test was the result.

Monsignor Ricci had gone a step further. It had always been thought that samples similar to the Turin Shroud should be tested before the crucial test itself. He was able to obtain samples of the relic, 'El Santo Sudario', from the Oviedo Cathedral in Spain. This image, little known outside the area of Oviedo, is a stained piece of linen which has been revered as a kind of pillow for the head of Jesus in the tomb. Dr McCrone prepared the two removed samples as he would do for the hoped-for Turin Shroud material. After the micro-analysis of the material by the sophisticated equipment in his Chicago facilities, a portion was made ready for carbon dating by Dr McCrone's preferred C-14 centre, the Lawrence Berkeley Laboratory in California. His analysis did not reveal anything noteworthy about this particular relic, and Lawrence Berkeley was unable to perform the carbon dating at this time because of a fault in their accelerator equipment.

Another set-back to having the carbon dating of the Shroud at an early stage was the interpretation of the results of an electron scanning of a thread of the Shroud taken by Princess Clotilde, when the backing was repaired in 1868. Professor Luigi Baima Bollone of Turin discovered a large amount of organic fungi (mould and mildew) on the examined thread which led him and others to worry that the same might be true of any samples of the Shroud. These fungi would, of course, contain carbon which, he thought, would preclude the possibility of obtaining a correct date for the relic. What Professor Bollone did not realise was that ultrasonic washing, followed by a purification of the cellulose of the prepared samples for C-14 testing, would remove all non-linen components.

In November 1977, the Archbishop of Turin announced the longest exposition of the Shroud to be held in modern times, and the first public one since 1933. It would occur from 27 August to 8 October 1978 and reach its climax in the first Sindonological Congress since 1950, bringing together all the leading experts on the relic.

Nothing was known of the fate of the 'New Mexico proposals' until 24, April 1978, when a communication issued from the Scientific Commission of the International Centre for Sindonology. This was the finalised version to be placed before the Archbishop. That he would accept was a foregone conclusion, but one item in the report was indefinitely postponed, namely, carbon dating, because the members of the Commission did not have '. . . a consensus among the experts on the 100% efficacy of the test in the specific case of the Shroud'. Most of the New Mexico proposals were accepted but it was the absence of the C-14 tests which created the most attention. What especially worried those of us asking for carbon dating was the fact that the Congress came at the end of the exposition and, if new samples might be needed in addition to those already removed (especially since one was from the sidestrip of the Cloth), the time of the Congress would be too late, since the relic would be returned to the reliquary. The whole procedure of obtaining the necessary material for the test would have to begin again.

With this in mind, I released the Turin communication to *The Times*, thinking that at least a brief mention of the situation might create a stimulus for the increasing number of people in Britain who were taking an interest in the Shroud's testing. *The Times* put the story 'Carbon 14 test rejected for Shroud', on the front page of its issue on 9, May 1978.

Two days later, Professor Harry Gove of the University of Rochester telephoned to say that his facilities were in a position to consider operating their new C-14 test as early as August 1978. Rochester is one of three North American laboratories using the new accelerator technique. The effort there has been a joint project with the University of Toronto and the General Ionex Corporation of Massachusetts.

Bringing the Turin Shroud to scientific testing has been a complicated and difficult process. The desire to let competent research go as far as possible in exploring the mysteries of this curious piece of Cloth has been hampered by a variety of vested interests and feelings. Some have felt that enough is already known – let the further mysteries remain. Others have wanted to approach its investigation under an aura of secrecy, giving the impression that certain results could be kept quiet, in case something damaging to the Shroud's authenticity is learned. In my opinion, an American Jesuit, Fr Francis Filas, presented the only scientifically defensible attitude to future investigation when he said at the New Mexico meetings: 'The rule for the Shroud study must be the search for truth and truth alone; . . . let the chips fall where they may, even though the finding of new objective truth may uncover new problems and new questions.'

Many of the attitudes towards testing the shroud assume a possible authentication in the future which no amount of research can ever produce. There will never be any final proof that the Turin

Shroud is the actual Cloth that wrapped the body of Jesus of Nazareth. Even if all the proposed tests further indicate that this object is not a forgery, as we know forgeries with paintings and historical artefacts, it can never be said that this is Jesus' burial cloth. Authenticating the Shroud is not like declaring a questionable painting to be genuine. Ultimately all that could be said is that it is a piece of linen of the time of Jesus and that the person it portrays was crucified in the manner that the Gospels say Christ was and that the image creating process seems to suggest an unusual combustion of radiant energy. This evidence is, of course, extraordinary. What other artefact contains such astounding information? Many Christians will arrive at one conclusion, having the full evidence before them. "It is the Lord!" (John 21.7). But this conviction, as always, must come through the eyes of faith.

Chapter Three

The Pathologist and the Shroud
J. Malcolm Cameron

The Gospel record nowhere implies that the Shroud in which Jesus Christ was wrapped after his Crucifixion revealed an image of his body, let alone his numerous wounds. The task of reconstructing the chain of events that link the Turin Shroud to Calvary is by no means easy. The Gospels recall how Christ was scourged, crowned with thorns, forced to walk perhaps some six hundred yards bearing the cross-beam of the cross, during which time he may have had numerous falls to the ground. Thereafter he was subsequently nailed to the Cross and later his side was pierced with a lance by a Roman sentinel.

I have been asked to comment on the image as a pathologist. Colour photographs of the Shroud indicate the body to be a sepia with a touch of yellow ochre hue, which appears so faintly when viewed that it can only be visible to the naked eye in certain conditions. The darker brownish marks in the body represent trickles of blood and/or serum issuing from the wounds. The outline of the figure stands out well in the black and white photographs taken by Giuseppe Enrie in 1931. The Cloth itself portrays a naked male corpse with hands crossed, and around the chin, supporting the lower jaw, is a *sudarium* – a napkin or handkerchief which passes across the beard and behind the hair. (See chapter five, page 73 f.). The position of the body as depicted on the Shroud is consistent with that of a crucified body in a state of post-mortem rigor (that is, muscle-stiffening after death whilst still on the Cross), which would naturally set in in the position into which the body would slip after death.

I agree entirely with my colleague, Dr Derek Barrowcliff, Home Office Pathologist and Medico-Legal Expert from Warwickshire, when he states that bodies do bleed after death for a period of time, but the Shroud does not show any smudging of the rivulets from the marks of the scourging, nor from the abrasions, particularly on the left knee. Blood, however, that has flowed during life and clotted on the skin may somehow have been transferred to the Cloth. It is not unknown for clots to undergo what is known as fibrinolysis as a result of enzymatic or bacterial action and could possibly be absorbed by linen; that is to say the blood would break down into numerous components and would be extremely difficult to differentiate.

The multiple puncture marks with attendant rivulets of blood over the scalp, extending from the centre of the forehead towards the front round to the level of the ears at the back of the head, would suggest a clump of thorny twigs being pressed down upon the head, rather than a circlet, which artists frequently symbolize as a 'crown of thorns'.

The image of the face is indicative of one who has suffered death by crucifixion and is not alive, for the linen cloth would act like a plastic membrane and would be sucked into the mouth and nostrils were the victim alive, as happens in tragic cases when a plastic bag is placed over the head of a child or adult resulting in death.

Reviewing the face, one can see several swellings and bruises over the facial areas, particularly the left cheek and forehead, under the right eye and across the nose, which could well be broken. The lower lip also gives the impression of having been swollen, injuries consistent with the face having come into contact with firm or hard surfaces during life; that is to say, with the victim either being struck in the face or falling on the face whilst carrying the beam of a cross. The eyes appear to be closed and sunken, suggestive that eye changes after death had occurred. There is no indication to suggest that any metallic coin or object had been placed over the eyes to keep them closed. The arms are bent and across the lower abdomen; this would, in my opinion, have been done forcibly in order to break the rigor or muscle stiffening of the shoulder-girdle – a not unusual problem when dealing with death from any cause, in order to get the body into a straight position. The track of the blood rivulets from the nail-marks of the wrists indicate fluctuation in the degree of sagging of the body on the cross during life. This varied from 55 to 65 degrees approximately.

Anatomical experiments carried out in 1940 stated that, in order to support the victim in crucifixion, the nails would need to have been driven into the wrists (carpal bones) and not the palms of the hands (between the meta-carpal bones) as has been depicted by artists throughout the ages. This mode of positioning of the nails in the wrists could damage the median nerve, causing the thumb to bend over the palm for, as can be seen from the image depicted on the Shroud, the thumbs are not seen. The image of the hands suggests the fingers to be somewhat shrivelled, indicative, in my opinion, of either deprivation of blood or post-mortem change.

The lance entering the chest cavity on the right side of the body in the fifth interspace, that is to say between the fifth and sixth ribs in an upward, inward direction, would penetrate the right lung, causing it to collapse, with resulting pneumothorax (i.e. air under pressure in the chest cavity) and subsequent bleeding from the lungs into the chest cavity and further penetration for some 8 to 9 inches (i.e. the length of the blade of a Roman lance) could well penetrate the principal chamber on the right side of the heart. Such a wound is frequently seen in domestic murder in the present day, resulting in almost immediate death resulting from bleeding into the chest cavity. A spear wound is visible in the Shroud itself just to the left of a triangular patch sewn on by the Poor Clares after the fire at Chambéry in 1532.

Examination of the upper back of the trunk reveals deep bruising of the shoulder blades, indicating the angle at which the cross beam of the cross might have been carried, but within this bruising there are marks of scourging. I agree entirely with Dr Bucklin's view that the scourge marks on the body would be consistent with a *flagrum*. Had the victim been a Roman citizen, he would have been beaten with rods, not whipped with the *flagrum* and, secondly, the inflicters of this punishment were not of the Jewish faith as their law forbade more than forty lashes.

I am also in total agreement with the views expressed by Dr Robert Bucklin and Dr Barbet that the nail fixing the feet passed between the metatarsal bones, that it to say the long bones of the foot, and not through the heel bone.

The image on the Shroud indicates to me that its owner – whoever he may have been – died on the cross, and was in a state of rigor, when placed in it. Even after the most extensive scientific and forensic tests, it is my belief that we shall only be able to prove the fact that the Turin Shroud *might* be the burial cloth of Jesus Christ, not that it actually *is*.

Chapter Four
The Shroud:
further scientific investigation
Stuart J. Fleming

Within a space of five years the Turin Shroud, as a Catholic relic, has moved from near obscurity into the limelight of human curiosity. The lay appetite has been much whetted by the documentary film, *The Silent Witness*. But sheer curiosity is not a criterion for authenticity of any artefact and that is exactly the problem the Shroud poses: is it authentic, in any sense of the word? Remember here that it is in no way sufficient to disprove it is a medieval fake produced just before de Charny exhibited it at Lirey. The claim laid out for investigation is whether this remarkably-marked length of linen is the burial sheet used in the entombment of Jesus. That claim is the basis for it being a vital relic. To the Christian, Jesus and Christ are synonymous: to the atheist, Christ means nothing, yet the very survival of a document of the experience of death of a major religious leader would still have its fascination.

The roots of distrust about the authenticity of the Turin Shroud, in the most elementary sense, are deep. We are told that the de Charny family offered no denial when the local bishops roundly condemned the Shroud as a fake and they made no attempt to explain how it came into their possession. Such an attitude scarcely inspires confidence that the Shroud is any different from the host of fraudulent relics then extant, other than being more elaborate. And I suppose the 'low-key' line taken by the authorities of Turin Cathedral, where the Shroud is presently kept, could be similarly regarded. The first serious investigators who were allowed access to the Shroud's fabric in November 1973 must have been fully mindful of the scepticism with which it was viewed outside the Catholic Church. They planned their strategy of analysis accordingly.

The principal elements of the technical information currently available on the Shroud can be seen as of two kinds, one direct (as derived from the 1973 samplings), the other indirect, such as the interpretation of the Shroud's image from a medical standpoint, (Chapter three). Let me summarize that information.

The Egyptologist, Silvio Curto, has established that the Shroud is *twill-weaved* (weft threads passing alternately under one and over two or more warp threads) and has made the observation that this technique of making linen probably originated in Syria or Mesopotamia some time before the second century AD. He also pointed out that the fabric incorporated some traces of cotton (presumably contaminant gathered up from the loom on which the Shroud was woven) and that the cotton fibre, in structure, corresponded to the type *Herbaceum* commonly used in the ancient Middle East.

Then, from between those threads, a Swiss criminologist, Dr Max Frei, has gathered data on the pollen remains trapped there insidiously over the centuries. Pollen grains are male reproductive structures produced by seed-bearing vegetation and every year they are shed in their thousands to travel far and wide on air currents and wind-flows. Nature's 'statistics' offer few chances of female plant fertilization, so by far the majority of the pollen grains fall to the ground, there to be worn down by microbiological activity until only the organic grain walls are preserved. However, those pollen 'shells' that survive are very much species – specific in their fine structure. Consequently Dr Frei could identify not only pollen originating from plants of Northern Europe (in keeping with the Shroud's known history in France and Italy) but also a few unusual intrusions, including distinctive *Halophytes* which, because of their special adoption of environments rich in salt, exist almost exclusively near the Dead Sea. Additionally a small suite of pollen grains produced positive evidence that the Shroud has spent some part of its history in the Anatolian Steppes of Turkey.

Separately, Giorgio Frache and his colleagues have put a great deal of effort in trying to trace any residues of blood in the vicinity of wounds indentified in the Shroud's image. Having established that the staining visible to the naked eye comprised red discoloration of only the outer parts of surface fibres, they proceeded with several chemical tests in a search for haemoglobin residues. In particular, peroxidase (a persistent component of blood) was sought by asking it to catalyse release of oxygen from hydrogen peroxide in the presence of benzidine which should have turned blue. It did not, even though the reaction is an extremely sensitive one. Then they looked for haematin (a haemoglobin derivative quite commonly retained in ancient stains) using a conventional soda/glycerine of potassium reaction. It was not there. Equally important however, this close scrutiny of the Shroud's very threads (admittedly only a few) indicated the complete absence of any pigments, confirming the views of others that the image was not *painted* onto the Shroud.

This last point was subsequently underwritten by the work of the two USAF physicists, Dr John Jackson and Dr Eric Jumper, who tackled the Shroud's image from a different angle. They had Giuseppe Enrie's 1931 photographs of the entire Shroud's surface and they had taken note of Paul Vignon's allusion (in *The Shroud of Christ* of 1902) that the intensity of the image seemed to vary inversely with the probable separation of the Shroud's surface and the contours of the body it had enclosed. Now, using a VP-8 Image Analyser, like that used in the United States Space programme to map out the contours of the Moon, they generated a three-dimensional relief with the body's profile showing a minimal distortion. (See chapter two, page 49f.).

Separate again, a strong medical lobby has grown that can interpret in minute detail almost every feature of the image in straightforward physiological terms, based on a limited amount of guesswork as to the trauma experienced by the human body before and during crucifixion.

Obviously the absence of pigments coupled with the three-dimensional quality of the overall image rules out any notion that a medieval forger deliberately set out to produce the Shroud. I have pondered whether it is too much of a chance that the Shroud should have appeared so soon after its alleged owner, Geoffrey de Charny, was felled at the battle of Poitiers by a lance-thrust. Was the image that of the good Geoffrey, after all? Was the fraud a thing that grew out of the image's chance production, the de Charny family only recognising the merits of the Shroud somewhat belatedly? I have pondered briefly too whether some parts (particularly the 'blood-stains') were late additions included to heighten the image's effect.

True, use of a fabric of Middle East origins was improbable but, given that it had been imported for quite separate reasons, the presence of pollen remains of similarly distant origins shrinks in significance. The pollen found is specific geographically, not chronologically. Additionally the only firm conclusion to be drawn from the research of Dr Jackson and Dr Jumper is that the image was not formed by a simple 'contact print' process: again there are no chronological implications in their analysis. Lack of blood residue in the relevant sections of the image does seem to rule out a tampering with the image after the significance of its basic form had been recognised, but, of course, that same lack of blood residue would put the authenticity of the Shroud in doubt whatever its dating might be.

It is the medical evidence that we are certainly looking at a gruesome document of crucifixion which satisfies me the Shroud is not medieval in origin. The single detail that the arm's wound is where it is, at the wrist (not through the palm, as depicted in paintings of the *Crucifixion* before the Shroud's emergence) is incentive enough to search further back in time for an alternative dating for the Shroud. But when? The prime target for future research must be the first to the fourth centuries AD. Before then the Roman practice of crucifixion involved tying the victim on the gibbet; crucifixion as a practice at all ceased during the reign of Constantine, *circa* AD 330.

There is only one reliable way to date organic remains scientifically. That is by the radiocarbon method. In the upper regions of the Earth's atmosphere some of the energy of cosmic radiation is constantly being utilised in the production of neutrons which can react with nitrogen through a reaction $^{14}N + n \rightarrow ^{14}C + H$ (^{14}C is radiocarbon). Initially the distribution of its atoms is non-uniform (the cosmic ray flux reaching the stratosphere is more intense at the Earth's poles than at the equator) but at about 10km above the Earth's surface circulating air currents soon mix up different parts of the atmosphere. In this way some 7.5 kg of ^{14}C is added to the world's carbon reservoir every year, about 1% of this being taken up by the plant and animal kingdoms of the biosphere. On land, plant life converts carbon dioxide into nutrients through photosynthesis so that the carbon becomes organically bound in a living organism. In their turn, the plants are food for animals so the ^{14}C gradually moves until, in a cycle which is completed only when the death of an organism results, eventually, in its decomposition, it is released in carbon dioxide re-absorbed into the atmosphere. However, any dead organic material (for example, the flax used in linen-making) that is left behind still contains some ^{14}C. Since this is no longer being replenished from the atmosphere, the concentration of the ^{14}C is gradually reduced by radioactive decay. Thus the death of the organism, when the intake of ^{14}C ceases, marks the 'time-zero' and thereafter the concentration present in a sample of material will decrease following the exponential law,

$$N = N_0 \exp(-t/\tau)$$

where N_0 is the initial number of atoms of ^{14}C, whose mean life period (τ), is 8270 years.

This equation is the basis of ^{14}C-dating. We know the present day concentration of ^{14}C in living organisms: it is close to 5.8×10^{10} atoms per gramme of total carbon. Assuming the rate of ^{14}C-

production throughout antiquity was constant,[1] this figure must be N_0 as well. Once N, the number of ^{14}C-atoms in an ancient artefact has been measured in the laboratory, the age of that artefact, t years, follows at once.

Until last year there was no direct way to measure the number of ^{14}C-atoms still in an ancient sample. The conventional approach in ^{14}C-dating developed by Willard Libby in the 1950's and based on the measurement of the *rate* of decay of the ^{14}C-content of an artefact has rightly taken its place as the most powerful means of scientific dating in archaeology. However it could never be considered seriously in solution of problems as sensitive as the authenticity of the Turin Shroud, since, conservatively speaking, it would have required destruction of close to a 100 cm^2 of the linen fabric. Today, however, the same answer might be achieved by analysis of just a few threads.

The cause of the dramatic improvement in the capacity of the ^{14}C-method has been the successful link-up of particle-accelerating systems to a highly sensitive mass spectrometer that can efficiently discriminate between atoms only shades apart in mass. For example, Richard Muller's group at the Lawrence Berkeley Laboratory in California, during their search for quarks (a component of each atomic nucleus, theoretically predicted but elusive in measurement), recognised that their cyclotron could be readily adapted for ^{14}C-analysis in this way. Having extracted the carbon atoms from a carbon dioxide source, they accelerate them to an energy of 60 million electron volts (MeV) and a charge state of 3+, then count them in a subtly designed detector that identifies unambiguously the nuclear mass and charge of the incoming particle. Although the current efficiency of the system is low (only one in every ten thousand ^{14}C-atoms put in are eventually recorded), it is still probably adequate for Shroud analysis. Roughly speaking, each linen thread, being cellulose ($C_6H_{10}O_5$), contains 0.16 milligrammes of carbon per centimetre of length, which is equivalent to 930 exp (-t/8270) ^{14}C-atoms/cm (detected). If the Shroud did date to the time of Jesus, a mere ten centimetres of

1. It was not, principally because the Earth's magnetic field has changed appreciably over the past millennia, but this has been very extensively studied (by calibration against tree-ring dating of various wood species: see Ralph. E.K. *et.al.,* 1973: *MASCA Newsletter 9,* page 1f). This aspect of ^{14}C-dating has little bearing on the main theme of discussion here; we need only note that it is possible to apply a correction for this factor.

thread would yield more than 7000 ^{14}C-atoms, the statistics on their counting (± 85 atoms) injecting only a matter of some ± 25 years uncertainty into the age calculation.[2]

There are other difficulties in this approach (most notably that of keeping the cyclotron chamber free of extraneous ^{14}C produced in separate nuclear experiments for which that accelerator was designed) that might broaden the uncertainty to a half century either way. There are also appreciable merits in the use of a Van der Graaff generator as the accelerating device, as illustrated by Harry Gove's group at Rochester (New York) and Erle Nelson's group at Simon Fraser University (see *Science 198*, page 507f), and it now seems certain that truly refined ^{14}C-analysis will only be achieved when a technical array has been set up, such as a system dedicated to dating work alone. [3] Be that as it may, the crucial point is that ^{14}C-dating has now advanced to a stage where it could answer one of the Shroud's mysteries – how old it is – accurately enough to influence the entire discussion of the artefact's history.

Whatever the date of the Shroud, the question still remains: how was the image on it formed? It is not a painting, so several of the kinds of analytical strategies that first spring to mind have little to recommend themselves. X-radiography may have ensnared Otto Wacker back in 1932, when he faked "Van Gogh" landscapes (the radiation had to penetrate thick layers of pigment to reveal how distinctive the master's method of painting composition was): resin analysis of a varnish may have established Hans van Meegeren's hand in the 'Vermeer' *Supper at Emmaus* which landed him in a Berlin court in 1945. However neither of these scientific notions can be relevant to the Shroud.

We are certainly not short of theories for the image's origins, the most popular being that the myrrh and aloes which would have been used in the conventional Jewish treatment of a burial sheet may have directly attacked the linen (in a chemistry involving ammonia) or may have reacted with morbid sweat to produce a form of oxidizing scorch-mark.[4]

2. The uncertainty quoted here is the so-called *standard deviation* (θ). For those readers not familiar with the term (and even scientists struggle with its concept at times!) I would refer them to my book, *Authenticity in Art*, page 144f.

3. See Hedges, R.E., 1978: *New Scientist 77*, page 599f.

4. Pier Luigi Baima Bollone has recently confirmed that fine indelible impressions on cloth can be produced in this way, producing a negative image of the kind on the Shroud.

Ray Rogers of the Los Alamos Laboratory tends to favour a thermal degradation process, on the basis of the similarity in colour between the principal image and the areas damaged in the Chambéry fire in 1532. There was also appreciable speculation on image formation that could result from radiation bursts, akin to a thermonuclear flash of energy or perhaps by a mechanism similar to flash photolysis involving fibre destruction by intense light.[5]

The only tangible facts we have on this matter are Frache's observations mentioned earlier (that the fibre discoloration is near-superficial on the linen fibres) and a hard reality that, to appear different to the human eye, the regions 'stained' (for want of a better description) and the linen matrix behind them must have different properties in terms of light absorption. In technical terms there have to be *colour centres* in the stain.

Formation of a colour centre in a cellulose is possible only by two mechanisms. Either an impurity element substitutes for one of the atoms of the normal molecular structure, its effect being to distort slightly that structure; or the molecular structure may be flawed, perhaps by disruptions of the normal sequence of atoms that leave them dangling, perhaps by localised re-organization into a new molecular form, each again causing strain effects in the bulk structure of the cellulose. The identification of impurities and the identification of structural flaws generally calls for different methods of fibre analysis.

My own inclination in the search for impurities is to suggest *autoradiography* of the whole Shroud as a precursor to more detailed thread-by-thread research. The principle here is that with quite low neutron fluxes (perhaps about 10^9 neutrons/cm^2.sec.), many elements can be activated to a minor level of radioactivity,[6] their subsequent decay back to the original stable state involving release of various forms of radiation which are characteristic of their atomic origins, in energy and radioactive mean life-time (τ).

Exposure of a photographic film at the fabric's surface at various times after initial activation would record elemental distribution. Certain of the lighter elements that would tend to fit into the cellulose structure most comfortably, such as sodium and potassium (and perhaps sulphur and chlorine) could be detected efficiently in this way, as would some heavier elements such as iron and manganese, if present. A Shroud image mapped out in just a

5. See *The Turin Shroud*, Ian Wilson, page 209f.
6. See Sayre, E.V., Lechtmann, H.N., 1968: *Studies in Conservation 13*, 161.

single chemical element would, indeed, be a fascinating spectacle.

Study of the distribution of individual elements in much finer detail on individual threads calls for use of an *ion microprobe* as Dr Walter McCrone suggested at the Albuquerque Conference in 1977, though I am not sure that an area of analysis even as small as this method can achieve (0.01 micron^2) is sufficient to indicate whether an element is incorporated in the fibre by a diffusion mechanism.

We now also have available the remarkably versatile technique of *Raman spectroscopy* which is capable of identifying both organic and inorganic molecules. Its underlying principle is that, whilst a molecule will normally scatter an incident photon off its structure without altering that photon's energy, a small fraction of the molecule/photon interactions is not so 'elastic'. Sticker collisions result in excitation of the fundamental vibration modes of the molecule (termed, for example, the 'CC stretch', the 'CH bend', etc.), the incident photon then losing or gaining a minute package of energy characteristic of the nature of that mode. Over the past decade, use of high intensity lasers (particularly the *argon ion form*), with their sharply defined photon energies, have allowed the weak spectral lines of Raman scattering to be readily resolvable alongside the far more intense line of elastic scattering. And, within the past year, an ultramicroanalytical form of the equipment has been developed which can handle samples only 10^{-12} gramme in weight.

If the normal cellulose structure of the Shroud's linen now incorporates any strange dye-stuff, any ammonia-based molecular configuration, any by-product of cellulose produced by heat (furfural, formaldehyde, etc.) or any elements from spices like aloes, Raman spectroscopy should find it. It is probably the right tool to use now in a fresh search for blood components (particularly chemically-stable porphyrins), as its sensitivity must be close to a thousand times greater than the methods used by Frache in 1973.

Technical interpretation of the Turin Shroud must necessarily stagnate unless the artefact itself is made accessible. Lack of that access will simply spawn yet more wild ideas about the method of its image formation. There must be a priority on a reliable ^{14}C-date, then a clearcut identification of what features, physical or chemical, characterise the image-marked regions of the Cloth.

Chapter Five

The Shroud and the New Testament
John A.T.Robinson

One of the things that shook my natural predisposition to scepticism about the Turin Shroud was precisely that it could not at all easily be harmonized with the New Testament accounts of the grave-clothes. I am not saying that it is incompatible with them but simply that no forger starting, as he inevitably would, from the Gospel narratives, and especially that of the fourth, would have created the shroud we have. Yet *if* it is genuine, it must make us look again at the biblical evidence. The Gospels are notoriously difficult to harmonize with themselves, let alone with what has been called this 'fifth gospel'. Nevertheless it may, I believe, help us to reconstruct the situation in a manner which I, at any rate, would never have arrived at, unless I had been prepared to take account of this extra-canonical witness. [1]

Let us begin with the burial of Jesus. This incidentally is one of the best attested of all historical facts about him. That Christ not only died and rose but was 'buried' is part of our earliest summary of the Christian faith in a letter written within twenty-five years of the Crucifixion, where Paul is appealing to tradition which he himself received from the Jerusalem church [1 Corinthians 15.3-4], probably within five years of it [cf. Galatians 1.18]. The burial is also narrated in all four Gospels [Matthew 27.57-61; Mark 15.42-47; Luke 23.50-56; John 19.38-42], with John's account almost certainly independent of the others, and it is mentioned in a sermon

1. I have deliberately not cluttered this chapter with footnotes to authorities ancient or modern for the positions I have adopted. Suffice it is to mention three treatments which refer to a wealth of other evidence: Edward A. Wuenschel. 'The Shroud of Turin and the Burial of Christ', *Catholic Biblical Quarterly* 7 (1945), 405-37, and 8 (1946), 135-78. Ceslas Lavergne, OP., 'La preuve de la resurrection de Jésus d'après Jean 20,7'; 'Le sudarium et la position des linges après la resurrection'; 'Le corps glorieux et la preuve que Jésus est ressuscité', *Sindon* 3 (1961), nos. 5 & 6.

André Feuillet, 'La découverte du tombeau vide en Jean 20, 3-10 et la foi au Christ ressuscité', *Esprit et Vie* 87 (1977), nos. 18 and 19, 257-66, 273-84.

summary in Acts, 'they took him down from the gibbet and laid him in a tomb' [Acts 13.29], which from the word *xylon* (wood or tree) almost certainly goes back to pre-Lukan sources [cf. Acts 5.30; 10.39; Galatians 3.13; 1 Peter 2.24]. The view that we can know nothing about the body of Jesus, because as the corpse of a condemned criminal it would have been dissolved in a lime-pit, is sheer dogmatic scepticism, flying in the face of all the evidence that it met no such fate. In fact, under Jewish law [cf. Deuteronomy 21.23], it should have been buried before sun-down in one of the two plots in Jerusalem specifically reserved for criminals (The Mishnah, *Sanh.* 6.5), and desire to remedy the concession of the pagan governor (especially to a non-relative in the case of a man condemned for high treason) *could* have supplied a motive for fanatical Jewish patriots, zealous for the law, to raid the tomb and transfer the body.

Following, therefore, the evidence we have, which is factual and circumstantial and not obviously subject to doctrinal motivation or suspicious alignment, there is multiple testimony for the tradition that the body of Jesus, released by Pilate at the request of Joseph of Arimathea, was taken from the cross late on the Friday afternoon [Matthew 27.57; Mark 15.42] and laid in a rock-tomb [Matthew 27.60; Mark 15.46; Luke 23.53] hitherto unused [Matthew 27.60; Luke 23.53; John 19.41]. By then, despite the proximity of the grave [John 19.42], Luke tells us in an odd but graphic phrase (*epephōsken* [23.54]) it was already starting to be what we should call 'lighting-up time', i.e. when the lamps were lit or, more probably, when the first stars became visible which marked the beginning of the Sabbath. Clearly there was no time, before further work became illegal and darkness set in, for more than the most preliminary attention to the corpse. According to Mark [15.46] Joseph had already bought a linen cloth (*sindon*) and in this he wrapped (*eneilēsen*) or according to Matthew [27.59] and Luke [23.53] folded (*enetylixen*) the body of Jesus. According to John [20.39-40] Joseph and Nicodemus 'bound' it (*edēsan*; though one uncial manuscript has 'wrapped', perhaps by assimilation to Mark) in *othonia*. This last is a word of uncertain meaning but it is best regarded as a generic plural for grave-clothes of unspecified material, though presumably linen. At any rate Luke, or his scribe, [in 24.12] uses *othonia* to cover what he had previously [23.53] described as the *sindon*.

John adds that a substantial mixture of myrrh and aloes, evidently a dry preparation in powdered or granule form like

70

incense, was brought by Nicodemus and put 'with' the clothing, presumably to serve as a temporary agent to arrest the effects of putrefaction until further attention could be given. One of the things specifically allowed by the Mishnah (*Shab.* 23.5) to be done for a corpse if need be on the Sabbath was to 'let it lie on sand that it may be the longer preserved'. The enormous quantity of material (100 lbs, though the Roman pound was only about three-quarters of ours) could be an exaggerated figure to bring out the generosity of the gesture, like the stress, in the earlier story of the anointing, on the vastly expensive flask of oil which the woman broke into [Matthew 26.6,9; Mark 14.3,5; John 12.3,5; cf. Luke 7.47]. But there are parallels for such quantities at the funerals of important personages, and if the mixture were packed under and around the body a good deal would have been needed. It is perfectly credible as a rich man's last tribute [cf. Matthew 27.57 and Isaiah 53.9].

Finally, all the evangelists agree, a stone was 'rolled across' the mouth of the tomb [Matthew 27.60; Mark 15.46; and by implication Luke 24.2 and John 20.1] for protection until the women could return some thirty-six hours later at first light on Sunday. Meanwhile, according to Mark [16.1], the women purchased aromatic oils when the Sabbath ended at nightfall on Saturday, precisely as the Mishnah lays down (*Shab.* 23.4). (Luke [23.56] has them prepare spices and perfumes early on the Friday evening before resting on the Sabbath). These were evidently in liquid form to 'anoint' the body of Jesus [Mark 16.1], just as before his death the woman had anointed it [Luke 7.38,46; John 12.3; cf. 11.2] by 'pouring' [Matthew 26.7; Mark 14.3] perfumed oil from her flask. The purpose of these unguents was different from that of the Johannine mixture. It was, after the obligatory washing of the corpse [cf. Acts 9.37], for which elementary act it is clear from the silence of all the canonical witnesses (in contrast with the later apocryphal Gospel of Peter, 24) there had been no time on the Friday, to clean it up and leave it in a decorous and fragrant condition. Normally of course this would have been done in preparation for entombment [cf. Matthew 26.12; Mark 14.8; John 12.7] rather than after it.

So far there is no difficulty in correlating the biblical evidence with that of the Shroud. Any presumption that the body was wrapped *round* in a winding sheet (contrast the swaddling cloths [Luke 2.7]) or swathed in 'strips of linen cloth' [John 19, 40, (New English Bible)], rather like an Egyptian mummy, is read into the texts (there is no compound in the Greek beginning with *peri,* round) and has no support in Palestine burial customs, which the

fourth evangelist insists were followed [John 19.40]. That the
corpse of Jesus was enfolded in a single linen cloth passing
lengthwise over the head and covering the whole body back and
front is not, I submit, what any forger with medieval or modern presuppositions would have thought of; but it makes complete sense of
the texts and fully comports with what other ancient evidence we
have.

It is when we come to the accounts of what was discovered on
Easter morning that the problems begin. According to Luke 24.12,
if it is part of the original text, as with a growing number of scholars
I am now persuaded that it is (it is omitted by only one Greek
manuscript), what Peter saw peering in was the *othonia,* which
must, as I said, mean or at least include the *sindon* Luke has
mentioned earlier [Luke 23.53]. According to John [20.5-8] 'the
other disciple' similarly 'peers in and sees the *othonia* lying', but
then Peter, followed subsequently by his companion, enters the
tomb and we are given a more detailed description. 'He sees the
othonia lying and the napkin (*sudarion*) which had been over the
head (*epi tes kephalés;* not 'about his head' as in the Authorised
Version) not lying with the *othonia* but folded or rolled
(*entetyligmenon*; the same word used earlier by Matthew and Luke
of the enshrouded body) in a place by itself (*choris . . .eis hena
topon*)'. The Greek is in fact extraordinarily elusive, considering the
significance that the evangelist evidently attaches to the details. His
expressions are so loose that it *could* mean that the clothes were
lying strewn about with the napkin that had been over the head
rolled up or bundled *into* a heap by itself. This would be entirely
compatible with Mary Magdalene's inference from the same
evidence [John 20.11] that the grave had been tampered with: 'they
have taken my Lord away, and I do not know where they have laid
him' [John 20.13]. So we should not expect the evidence of the eyes
to be of unambiguous interpretation. It was only the faith of one
man that put two and two together.

But what does the evangelist intend his readers to suppose that
the disciples did see? This cannot be decided without taking into
account his earlier description of the raising of Lazarus. His tomb
was a cave with a stone placed against it (*ep' auto* [John 11.38])
and he 'came out' from it 'bound (*dedemenos*) hand and foot with
bands (*keiriai*) and his face bound round (*periededeto*) with a
napkin (*sudarion*)' [John 11.44]. The New English Bible translation
'his hands and feet swathed in linen bands' is again a paraphrase.
There is nothing to say what the *keiriai* were made of — the only

ancient evidence (the scholiast on Aristophanes' *Birds*, 816) tells us that a *keiria* was 'a kind of binder made of twisted rushes, somewhat like a thong, with which bedsteads were strung'. All we know is that they restricted, though evidently not totally, the movement of the man's hands and feet. On the assumption (too obvious to mention) that Lazarus had also been placed in a shroud, it would seem likely that the thongs had been tied loosely round the outside of it to hold it in place, functioning in this respect in lieu of a box (which the Jews did not use until the body decomposed and the bones were put together in an ossuary). This is presumably what the women would have done to the body of Jesus after they had finished their work. The fact that they had not finished would explain the absence of any mention of *keiriai* in his case.

But what of the *sudarion* which was 'round the face' of Lazarus and 'over the head' of Jesus? *Sudarion* is a loan word from the Latin and defines the object not by its material (though clearly it was cloth of some kind) but by its function, namely to remove sweat, like a neckerchief or handkerchief – and so it is used elsewhere in the New Testament [Luke 19.20; Acts 19.12]. It seems in the highest degree improbable that a cloth for this purpose would have been big enough to cover the length of a man twice. It is clearly distinguished by John from the main body of the *othonia*, which Luke equates with the *sindon*. The only reason for supposing, as some have, that the *sudarion* is itself the Shroud is that the latter evidently did go over the head and face, as well of course as over the whole body. Yet neither in the case of Lazarus nor in that of Jesus does it say that the *sudarion covered* the face. We are told that it was round the face of the former and over the head of the latter. The only position, I submit, which fits both these descriptions, assuming as we surely must that they are referring to the same burial custom, is of something tied across the top of the head round the face and under the chin. In other words it describes a jaw-band, which would have been functionally necessary to keep the mouth shut and, together with the closing of the eyes [cf. Genesis 46.4], would have been required before *rigor mortis* set in. Reference is specifically made to these customs again in the Mishnah (*Shab.* 23.5), and the chin could be bound (though not the eyes closed) on the Sabbath, providing it was 'not in order to raise it but to prevent it sinking' (for movement of any sort was 'work'). The band was evidently constructed by folding or rolling diagonally a large handkerchief or neck-cloth, rather like our triangular bandage.

I began by assuming that the only trace that the *sudarion* could possibly have left on the enveloping *sindon* was at the top of the head, where I took the white strip in a negative image of the Turin Shroud to be the space for it. But with the realization from the three-dimensionality of the image revealed by the computer that the white spots are the high spots, I can now see that this is more likely to be a protruding ridge formed by the *sudarion* itself. Conversely the dark band immediately under the chin, especially when seen in '3-D', looks as if it is where the jaw-band has retracted a portion of the beard which would otherwise show up. The vertical dark strips on either side of the face between the cheeks and the locks, otherwise so odd, could similarly be caused by the band holding back the intervening hair. The band would then continue up in front of the ears, behind the hair growing from the forward part of the head, and be knotted over the crown. So if I am right, the line of the jaw-band would be reflected on the Shroud, not only by where it directly touches it, but still more by what it retracts and thus does not allow to show up.

That the *sudarion* was a jaw-band has been recognised by a number of commentators from the New Testament material alone and would seem to me almost certain. It is an altogether more likely interpretation of the Johannine evidence than that it refers to some purely hypothetical turban-like object collapsed in upon itself such as Henry Latham supposed in the famous chapter on the witness of the grave-clothes in his influential book *The Risen Master* (1901). This would be described as going 'round the head', which John does not say of Jesus (despite the Authorised Version), and could not be said to go 'round the face', as he does of Lazarus. But though the Turin Shroud is not itself required to establish this point, it has certainly helped me to envisage more clearly what the function and position of the *sudarion* must have been. This again is not, I suggest, how any forger would have thought. He would have imagined it lying over the face, rather like the bogus St Veronica's veil and incorporated its image on a separate piece of material.

But in what position are we to suppose that the *sudarion* was subsequently found? This depends on what picture the fourth evangelist is intending to present. That he means us to conclude that the grave had been rifled and the body removed from the clothes (as his expressions would *allow*) is clearly impossible: this first and most natural explanation is firmly corrected. Does he intend us to suppose that the grave-clothes had been left behind undisturbed in their original positions, the body having passed through and out of them, as Latham argued? Like most people, I find today, I had always assumed that this was his intention; but I am not so sure. He *could* of course have imagined the body passing through the clothes as later it did through closed doors [John 20.19, 26] – though why then had the stone been removed [John 20.1]? But dematerialization is, I suspect, a distinctively twentieth-century way of envisaging the relationship between flesh and spirit, matter and energy. How a first-century Jew would naturally have envisaged resurrection would have been as a corpse 'awaking from sleep', like Tabitha in Acts [9.40], as indeed Jesus predicts of Lazarus [John 11.11], and then like Lazarus 'coming out' of the tomb. The difference was that whereas Lazarus, returning to the weakness of a flesh-body, had to have the stone taken away and the bands untied, Jesus would have been conceived as divesting himself and 'walking out' on death. Something like this seems to have been imagined by the apocryphal Gospel according to the Hebrews, where Jesus hands the *sindon* to the servant of the (high?) priest, a story which, however legendary, reflects the presuppositions of the ancient world.

The same assumption seems to have been true of almost all exegetes until recent times. Thus Chrysostom makes the point that the arrangement of the grave-clothes argues not that they had not been moved but that it could not have been the work of robbers, who would either have taken them with the body or left them in disarray. Bengel, the great eighteenth-century commentator, says that it means that they were not 'thrown off in a disorderly manner: the angels doubtless ministered to the rising man, one of them composing the linen cloths, the other the napkin'! Godet at the end of the nineteenth century says, 'the napkin especially, wrapped together carefully put aside, attested not a precipitate removal, but a calm and holy awakening'; and Westcott takes the same line.

One is bound to admit that the tidiness of the arrangement lies more in the eye of the beholder than in the Greek. But, if the clothes had been left undisturbed, the jaw-band would *not* have been separated from the rest in a place apart, but have been *between* the two layers of the *sindon*. To attempt, with Lavergne (and, with modifications, Feuillet) to make the Greek mean that the *sudarion* was 'on the contrary wrapped (in the shroud) in its (original) position' is a desperate expedient. If this is what the evangelist meant to say, his language is not merely loose but positively misleading. I think indeed that he intends us to infer that, while the *othonia* were lying flat, the *sudarion* was still in its twisted oval shape (as it could have been, however removed). But that the latter was found *inside* the former is an impossible deduction. If, as Latham surmised, the *sudarion* was a separate head-piece (for which there is no evidence in Jewish burial customs of the time) and if the *othonia* were strips of linen that covered only the body, then undisturbed the two could have been separated by the distance of the neck. But if, as all the evidence suggests, the *sudarion* was a jaw-band and the *othonia* corresponded to the *sindon,* and to the Shroud we have, then I think the conclusion must follow that, for the two to be found lying apart, movement of some sort would have been involved, (as *eis hena topon*, 'into one place', would strictly suggest though not, in this Greek, necessarily imply).

None of this is of course to say anything about what actually occurred. On this a reverent agnosticism alone is appropriate. The canonical gospels are silent, in contrast again with the Gospel of Peter (35-44) which describes Jesus rising from the tomb supported and held by the hand by two men whose heads reached to heaven, with the cross following! All the Shroud can do is to confirm, as I believe it does, the presuppositions of first-century as opposed to twentieth-century readers. But finally what *difference* would it make to us if it were genuine?

First let me stress the 'if'. There will never be final proof that this is the actual cloth that wrapped the body of Jesus of Nazareth. Even if all the tests proved positive there would only be a very strong possibility that it was the burial cloth of this man. If the date of the linen were to come out correct, then there is a pretty powerful concurrence of evidence that would point to this conclusion. Clearly it carries the image of a man, almost certainly a Jew, of the right age, who suffered death by crucifixion. Though most of the marks of this barbarous punishment would not point distinctively to this one man, the evidence of severe injury to the scalp by a 'crown of thorns' surely cannot reasonably be posited of any usual victim: it was a mock coronation as King of the Jews. There is also the fact that, unlike any other shroud, it did not disintegrate with the corpse it covered. For some reason it became separated from its body prior to decomposition and was regarded by a long series of people in most hazardous circumstances as valuable enough to preserve. If then everything else were to prove positive, there must be a strong presumption that it belonged to this man. We cannot say more, but neither, I think, can we say less. If then it were this very cloth, what difference would it make?

In the first place it would be bound to make us take the evidence that comports with it much more seriously. There is, as we have seen, the evidence from the Mishnah which agrees at points very well, and which for the first time would be confirmed as valid of Judaea prior to the war of 66-70 AD. Then there is the archaeological evidence from the skeleton found in Jerusalem in 1968 of a Jew named Jehohanan, crucified at this same period, which confirms (apparently) that the nails did not, as Christian tradition has depicted and a forger would have assumed, go through the palms, which medical tests have shown in any case could not support the weight of the body. But it is the bearing out of the New Testament evidence that is much the most significant. It does not of course prove the Gospels are, or set out to be, exact historical records. The well-known differences between them remain, though I am convinced that the light thrown by the Shroud can help us to understand how apparently discrepant accounts e.g., of the grave-cloths, are in fact compatible.

The first thing that the genuineness of the Shroud would shake is the theory that the whole story of the empty tomb is an invention of the early church. Despite its advocacy by Bultmann and other distinguished scholars I have never regarded this in any case as in the least degree probable. The story is firmly entrenched in all the strands of the Gospel tradition, and I believe that Paul's statement of the common apostolic teaching, received after his conversion, that Christ 'was buried . . . and was raised to life on the third day' points to a connection between the Resurrection and the tomb (not merely the appearances) which takes us back to the very first years of the Christian movement. The survival of the shroud would simply add weight to the very strong presumption that the tomb of Jesus *was* found empty – though how it became empty neither the Gospels nor, I believe, the Shroud tell us. But somehow the body disappeared. The traditional challenge, that the authorities had only to produce the body to discredit the whole message that Jesus was risen, must, I think, be taken more seriously than I have tended to suppose. The argument certainly does not hold the other way round. The mere fact that it was not produced can never prove it could not have been produced, any more than the absence of Hitler's corpse to this day proves that he rose from the dead. But if a lifeless cadaver had been produced which could irrefutably have been identified with Jesus of Nazareth, then the proclamation that he was not dead but alive would have seemed as unconvincing to Jewish as to modern presuppositions. The Christian church would never have got off the ground. Positively this proves nothing about the mode or meaning of 'resurrection'. But the Shroud unquestionably adds weight to the universal witness of the New Testament that there was a physical and not merely a spiritual aspect to this event.

If genuine, the Shroud would also constrain us to take more seriously many details in the record which its image had confirmed. This applies especially to the fourth Gospel – a conclusion which does not surprise me in the least, since I have become convinced that it contains some of the best history in the New Testament. But it should shake a good many current scholarly presuppositions that it tells us much of the Christ of faith but little of the Jesus of history.

First, in regard to the death of Jesus, the Shroud bears out the reports in all the Gospels of multiple buffetings and Roman scourgings (far exceeding the Jewish thirty-nine strokes) and confirms how brutal these were. It supports a cap, and not merely as traditional art would have suggested, a circlet of thorns. The additional abrasions on the back of one shoulder could also bear out the tradition which John records [19.17], though not the Synoptists, that Jesus was compelled to carry his own cross at least part of the way. Again, the attachment of the body to the cross by nails, and not ropes, attested by John [20.25] and implicitly by Luke [24.39] is of course also confirmed by the Shroud. So are two important details strongly insisted upon by John on the evidence of eye-witness. The first is that the legs of Jesus were not broken, unlike those of the two crucified with him [John 19.32-3], a practice now confirmed by the mangled skeleton to which I have referred. The second is the lance-stab in the side with its effusion of blood and water which is clearly traceable on the Shroud [John 19.34].

With regard to the burial and grave-clothes, we have already seen that the Gospel evidence, though most unlikely to have suggested the Shroud we have, both illumines and is illuminated by it at a large number of detailed points, not least in regard to the *sudarion* of which again John alone speaks.

Finally, though this is inevitably a subjective judgement, the image of the Shroud reveals a visage, like that of Hamlet's father, altogether 'most majestical'. It is surely a face that could credibly have commanded the loyalty and faith which the Gospels describe. The image might have been terribly disillusioning. But no one, I think, since its full photographic likeness became revealed, from the agnostic Delage onwards, could say that it was out of keeping with the man of supreme inner authority whom the Gospel records present.

Yet the face on the Shroud, we should never forget, is the face of a dead man. Its exclusive picture is a last testimony to the past. It is the imprint of the old body of flesh and blood, not of the risen Christ, nor even apparently, from its closed eyes, of some moment of awakening. Even if the cloth is authentic, it could still have been removed from the corpse by human agency after the image had been formed. Yet, on what looks at present to be the most promising hypothesis, it does appear to record some moment, some burst perhaps of low-energy non-ionizing radiation, lasting but a fraction of a second. Otherwise it would have penetrated further than the surface of the fibres, which is what the microscope tests disclose.

What then was this moment or this energy? No one can say – or perhaps ever will. We may, however, rule out dematerialization in the crudely literal sense that the entire mass of matter composing the body was changed, according to the formula $E = Mc^2$, into an equivalent amount of energy. That would have destroyed the Shroud, Jerusalem, and everything else one can think of. Matthew's 'violent earthquake' [28.2] would have been nothing! We are not here in the realm of transforming physical matter into physical energy according to the rules of repeatable experiment. If we can say anything at all, it seems that we are moving much more in the shadowy realm of paranormal physics and psychology associated with exceptionally intense spiritual states. The Gospel narratives – and we must do them the justice of starting by taking them seriously – speak of some other body, of spirit *not* of flesh (like the resuscitated body of Lazarus and the others), which could nevertheless appear to 'materialize'. What relation, if any, it bore to the 'astral' or other bodies of which parapsychology speaks, we cannot say. In the language of the men of the New Testament it would be a body of 'glory' or 'light' or 'spirit', such as that of the angels at the tomb, perceptible only to the eye of faith and vision. (Compare especially the description of the angel [Matthew 28.3] with that of the risen Christ [Revelation 1.14]). In other words, if we are to use any term at all, it would be one more like 'transmaterialization'. The New Testament accounts of the appearances differ considerably – though the degree of materialization and the difference of location seem to me neither here nor there and, like any other phenomena in this field, would depend greatly on the experiencing subject. In any case this is *not* the body which the Shroud shows us. What it *could* show us might be, so to speak, a side-effect of its generation, a brief but intense discharge of some sort of physical radiation sufficient to have left marks of thermal discoloration on the cloth. It would be the last trace, the final foot-print, as it were, of the old body – corresponding more to the skin sloughed off by the snake, except of course that it was nothing sub-stantial but only an image. For on the assumption of some kind of physical transformation, of which science as yet can say nothing, then all the material of the old appears to have been 'used up', in Professor Moule's phrase, in the creation of the new. There was nothing left over, not even hair and finger-nails, as in the striking parallels of Buddhist holy men quite literally 'absorbed into the light' which I quoted in my book *The Human Face of God* (p. 139). Of Jesus we must say unequivocally with the angelic messengers, 'he is not here' [Mark 16.6; Matthew 28.6]: it is vain to 'search among the dead for one who lives' [Luke 24.5] – even in the Shroud.

The Turin Shroud can provide no knock-down proof of Resurrection, and faith would surely not wish to have it so. We cannot even, in my judgement, usefully say whether it presupposes, let alone catches, some 'moment of resurrection'. For that is to compare one unknown (the process of the image-formation) with another (what we mean by 'resurrection'). It would not, if authentic, put anything beyond either faith or doubt. But it must surely make us less dismissive. We shall have to come to terms with the new evidence, however disturbing to our presuppositions scientific or religious. Indeed it should help to teach us, like any other advance in knowledge, that the more we know the more we do not know. It may humble us to confess that, in the words of my great Puritan namesake, John Robinson, 'God hath yet more truth to break forth' from his holy Shroud. It would not affect my faith, but it could affect my unbelief. For if in the recognition of the face and the hands and the feet and all the other wounds we, like those who knew him best, are led to say, 'It is the Lord!' [John 21.7], then perhaps we shall have to learn to count ourselves also among those who have '*seen* and believed'. But that , as St. John makes clear, brings with it no special blessing [John 20.29], but rather special responsibility [John 17.18-21].

Chapter Six

The Shroud of Jesus: icon and relic

Alberic Stacpoole, O.S.B

If the Turin Shroud is what it purports to be, then it is the ultimate icon of Jesus Christ in our midst. St. Paul, when he was confronted by the Athenian Epicurean and Stoic philosophers, challenged them with these words: 'Men of Athens, I have seen for myself how extremely scrupulous you are in all religious matters, because I noticed, as I strolled round admiring your sacred monuments, that you had an altar inscribed: To An Unknown God. Well, the God whom I proclaim is in fact the one whom you already worship without knowing it' [Acts 17. 22-23].[1] Paul is saying more to the Athenians than that a valid link can be established between their altar and the Christian faith: he is declaring once again that the Father, hidden from us in unapproachable light would remain an Unknown God had he not been interpreted to us by the Logos, the Word uttered by the Father himself as self-communication to creation, which cannot know him face to face till it attains worship in Spirit. Thus meanwhile, God being Spirit, Christ is the image of the invisible God [Colossians 1.15].

So it was that the Father uttered his perfect manifestation: 'In our own time, he has spoken to us through his Son ... He is the radiant light of God's glory and the perfect copy of his nature' [Hebrews 1.2-3]. The Word is the Wisdom of God; the Logos is light from Light Invisible, radiance of the Father's heart, impression of the Father's seal. The glory on the face of Christ is, Paul tells us, the illumination of the knowledge of God's glory which has shone upon our minds, the lighting of the invisible which is eternal. 'For it is not ourselves that we are preaching, but Christ Jesus as the Lord. It is the same God that said, 'Let there be light shining out of darkness', who has shone in our minds to radiate the light of the knowledge of God's glory, the glory on the face of Christ' [2 Corinthians 4.5-6].

So it is that we have the mind of Christ, Christ who is the Mind of God; we belong to Christ, and Christ belongs to the Father. For, as he said at his farewell discourse, 'No one can come

1. The Bible texts in this chapter are taken from The Jerusalem Bible.

to the Father except through me. If you know me, you know my Father too' [John 14.6-7]. 'The Father and I are one' [John 10.30]. In that sense, and it is the highest sense and the most intense, Christ is the icon of the unseen Light, to us on earth the only perceivable form and tangible substance of what is otherwise altogether beyond our perception. He alone mediates to man another world of being, the ultimate form of existence (some would say, 'beyond existence'), which without this mediation would remain ever incomprehensible to man's consciousness. Jesus Christ is therefore the only possible icon of the reality of God.

All created icons – created either in man's mind or by his hands – are but an obscure figure of the true icon; they are crude but not wholly ineffectual reminders of the one icon, Christ the Son. In a sense man himself, wounded and sinful as he is, infirm but seeking grace and able to receive grace as no other creature can, is an imperfect icon of the God who created him, in some dim analogous way a resemblance of Himself. A man of grace is a reflection of God. As Paul put it: 'We, with our unveiled faces reflecting like mirrors the brightness of the Lord, all grow brighter and brighter as we are turned into the image that we reflect; this is the work of the Lord who is Spirit' [2 Corinthians 3.18].

At an altogether lower level, but in the same order of thinking, man may create for himself icons which can remotely convey to him the shadow of the reality of the One Icon. The icon tradition runs through the whole history of the Church from its earliest catacomb emblems – holy images which grew into a specific pictorial language of icons, most richly developed in the Byzantine world and the Eastern Orthodox Church. The Church's icons have been marked by their catacomb origins, as frontal, laconic and lacking much depth-shadow. Our most ancient surviving icons date back to the fifth century; and in the writings of St. Basil, St. Gregory of Nyssa, and in the *Church History* of Eusebius of Caesarea, there is ample evidence from an earlier period. Indeed an apocryphal *Vita* of St. John the Evangelist takes the tradition back to the second century. All such icons of Christ, or his Blessed Mother, or a saint of special local significance are believed to be channels of divine blessing, or healing of body and spirit, for the faithful; and thus it is that they are painted by men of marked holiness after ample and elaborate preparation of spirit as well as skill. Icons have come to represent in their limited way man's participation in the divine life; for they share, however remotely, in the sanctity and glory of their prototype, vessels of the grace available to holy people living before God.

Now suppose that the One Icon, Jesus the Son, only satisfactory image of the Father, were to leave us his own icon not made by human hands. Suppose he left us an impression of himself as Son of Man at the moment when he had said 'It is achieved', that is, the moment when the redemptive act had been accomplished for all mankind, would we not then have at last – however inadequately – what the artists have sought to reach up to over two millennia, an icon done in perfect human likeness of the Christ, an icon done not with the highest of natural skills but by the power of the supernatural? And if this were so, would we not be seeing the finger of the divine tracing its character upon what man is alone able to grasp, an image fit for the senses to perceive and the intellect to rejoice over? If this were so, would we not expect to find that priceless icon surviving through the vicissitudes of earthly history and kept in open veneration in the heart of the Church as a constant inducement to prayer, and reminder of the central act of the Icon of God for men? Suppose, to make the leap from the tangible to the conceptual, that we have just such an icon of the Icon of the omnipotent God, in the Shroud of Turin: were that so, that then would be perhaps the most precious evidence and art on earth – not made by human hands but by the creativity of God.

Nor is this all. There are two traditions in the Church over the long years, the East settling for symbolism with the mind of poetry, and the West with a more practical mind settling for the tangible. The strong equivalent tradition of the rationalising Church of Western Europe and its worldwide missions has been a veneration of relics – either the very bones and bodies of the saints, or their clothes and possessions, or, more remotely, vessels and garments that have touched the primary relics of those martyrs and saints. The word 'relic' comes from the Latin *reliquiae* or mortal remains after the saint's *transmigratio* to the bosom of the Father, such remains having been honoured from the earliest time in the Church. Even when St. Paul was alive, for instance, so singular were the miracles done through him by God that 'when handkerchieves and scarves that had touched his skin were carried to the sick, they were rid of their diseases and evil spirits' [Acts 19.12].

As veneration of relics grew and liturgical cult grew with it, so all this began to be given theological justification through recourse to the doctrine of the mystical body. The martyrs' tombs, concentrated in a few places, were opened for their relics which were then distributed in the form of *brandea* (or objects that had touched the actual body of a saint) to the Church at large – some of such *brandea* being set up in reliquaries and others even hung round the neck in small cases to remind a Christian of the standards of sanctity of the martyr invoked, and to stimulate the living to similar devotion. The pursuit of relics reached such a pitch that the fathers of the Council of Carthage in 401 commanded that churches where no relic was honoured should be pulled down.

It was the belief of the Eastern Church that the soul was wholly present in any part of the body and that every part enjoyed the vital power of the whole body; and this added a force of argument to the veneration of relics. In the East, saints' bodies were made up into elaborate reliquaries which were then transported from place to place for solemn ceremonies. Naturally the great cities of Constantinople, Alexandria and Antioch became progressively enriched by such collections taken from lesser sanctuaries. Western practices inhibited such wanderings and gatherings, the Theodosian Code strictly penalising the spoliation of graves. Any translation of relics was rare, and only for serious reasons, at least until the Carolingian age when the acclaim of relics – even *brandea* – grew so considerable as to influence the economic and cultural development of society.

The cult of relics was introduced to the newly Christianised races (such as the Saxons of the north) as a useful way of overturning their cult of old idols and preventing them from reverting to such a cult. A need for relics arose all over Europe; and the catacombs came to be regarded as an inexhaustible mine for martyrs' bones. In the ninth century a trading corporation was formed specialising in the procuring and distribution of relics all over the continent. The greatest plunder and transportation of major relics occurred in 1204, when the Latin armies sacked Constantinople, the Shroud being one of the prizes to leave Byzantium for the West.

Veneration of relics enhanced the great cathedral and monastery pilgrim shrines (notably at Canterbury), determined the long pilgrim routes of the medieval world (notably to Santiago in Compostela), encouraged the exaltation of new church sanctuaries, prompted the proliferation of feasts and festivals (part ritual, part civic), and influenced the prolongation of liturgies and offices. The theologians felt called upon to speak about it all, and so St. Thomas Aquinas referred to the saints as sons and friends of God, able to intercede for the living in a special way. Relics, records and sensible signs of the holy, he wrote, related closely to Christ and to the

Father, being thereby fitting instruments for God's miracles. Lacking power within themselves, they yet 'excite to love by signifying the love that is achieved through the relic' (*Summa Theol.* 3a.5.6). Interestingly to our purpose, Aquinas argued that relics deserve more reverence than do images.

But we here do not need to make that choice. For where the icon tradition reaches its apex of wonder and awe *is* where the tradition of relics reaches its most holy tangible height – in the burial shroud of Jesus Christ (if we grant the leap of faith and accord authenticity to the Turin Shroud). The image of God comes to us from nowhere else in visual form. The body of Christ Risen left no direct relics. But on its most intimate clothing, the burial cloth or *sindon,* at the most intimately human moment, death and the hours following, the naked body of our Saviour left us his icon. There, on that awesome cloth, is the quintessential meeting place of the two ecclesial traditions, Eastern and Western. There lies before us the holiest icon upon the holiest relic.